Microsoft Power BI Quick Start Guide

Build dashboards and visualizations to make your data come to life

Devin Knight
Brian Knight
Mitchell Pearson
Manuel Quintana

BIRMINGHAM - MUMBAI

Microsoft Power BI Quick Start Guide

Commissioning Editor: Amey Varangaonkar
Acquisition Editor: Reshma Raman
Content Development Editor: Mohammed Yusuf Imaratwale
Technical Editor: Sushmeeta Jena
Copy Editor: Safis Editing
Project Coordinator: Hardik Bhinde
Proofreader: Safis Editing
Indexer: Rekha Nair
Graphics: Jason Monteiro
Production Coordinator: Aparna Bhagat

First published: July 2018

Production reference: 1280718

Published by Packt Publishing Ltd.
Livery Place
35 Livery Street
Birmingham
B3 2PB, UK.

ISBN 978-1-78913-822-1

www.packtpub.com

mapt.io

Mapt is an online digital library that gives you full access to over 5,000 books and videos, as well as industry leading tools to help you plan your personal development and advance your career. For more information, please visit our website.

Why subscribe?

- Spend less time learning and more time coding with practical eBooks and Videos from over 4,000 industry professionals

- Improve your learning with Skill Plans built especially for you

- Get a free eBook or video every month

- Mapt is fully searchable

- Copy and paste, print, and bookmark content

PacktPub.com

Did you know that Packt offers eBook versions of every book published, with PDF and ePub files available? You can upgrade to the eBook version at www.PacktPub.com and as a print book customer, you are entitled to a discount on the eBook copy. Get in touch with us at service@packtpub.com for more details.

At www.PacktPub.com, you can also read a collection of free technical articles, sign up for a range of free newsletters, and receive exclusive discounts and offers on Packt books and eBooks.

Foreword

The teams at Pragmatic Works that I have known over the last decade have been on top of all the latest trends in the Microsoft Business Intelligence world. Looking around my office and home, I located four books I have purchased that are authored by Pragmatic Works employees. The have produced Microsoft employees and independent consultants, as well as some of the most popular speakers at data conferences. Brian Knight founded Pragmatic Works, and I have never been bored in any of his sessions over the years. Devin Knight has leads a team of online content producers that is second to none. Mitchell Pearson has a brilliant way of presenting BI topics with their online learning and instructions. Manual Quintana has a strong personality that enables him to be an effective speaker.

This awesome team has developed a wonderful book to help Power BI users navigate a frequently changing product. However, they have formatted the book to help more experienced users jump to any chapter to learn about a new feature of Power BI. The flow is very intuitive and highlights the necessary guidance for all types of Power BI users. The book follows a step-by-step method for learning about Power BI with examples along the way. I really like when they give credit to a data platform community member for the work done and links to their information.

This book begins nicely with the introduction to the most important step in using Power BI—Get Data. Without data and the proper format, the visualizations are useless. The examples are of the most popular data structures that are used with Power BI. The second chapter focuses on the Query Editor (Power Query) with clear examples. The R language is explored via an interesting example. There is a simple explanation of the M language that helps the chapter flow to Native Queries.

The next section, about data modeling, comes at the perfect time. Data modeling has to be one of the biggest areas for new users. When explaining relationships, the writers do a nice job relating these complex topics to newbies. I really like the usability section examples for cleaning up the model, such as building hierarchies and sorting by a different column. Leveraging DAX is a great continuation from data modeling. Here, we learn some basic functions that are almost always used; plus, we get the time intelligence section for advanced slicing and dicing.

After all that, we get to the fun stuff—visualizations. The book breaks down the visualizations into sections that explain where each visualization is most useful. This is the right thing to do. There are so many types of charts that someone new can get really confused. I enjoyed the beginnings of chapters, where the application work space is labeled with explanations. The stroytelling chapter takes the visuals and places them in a format to help an end user understand the data being visualized. The book does a great job in expanding the concepts of the helpfulness of data, once formatted.

Of course, it does not stop there. Cloud deployments are discussed in the next chapter. This is the area where end users get to interact with the data but not modify the dashboard. The last chapter concludes with Power BI Report Services. This helps the users of Power BI who need to deploy to a local environment. Having this chapter directly after the one on gives the readers an understanding of the flexibility Microsoft has so graciously given us.

The authors have done an A+ job with this book. If you are a beginner, start at the first chapter. If you are intermediate user, go to the chapter with the topic that you need more information or examples on. If you are a manager, go to the last two chapters to find out where these visualizations can be deployed in your company. Providing data and step-by-step usage of that data in one package, this book is a must have for Power BI users.

Thomas LeBlanc

Data Warehouse Architect & Microsoft Data Platform MVP, Data on the Geaux

Contributors

About the authors

Devin Knight a Microsoft Data Platform MVP and the Training Director at Pragmatic Works. At Pragmatic Works, Devin determines which courses are created, delivered, and updated for customers, including 10+ Power BI courses. This is the seventh SQL Server and Business Intelligence book that he has authored. Devin often speaks at conferences such as PASS Summit, PASS Business Analytics Conference, SQL Saturdays, and Code Camps. He is also a contributing member to several PASS Virtual Chapters. Making his home in Jacksonville, FL, Devin is the Vice President of the local Power BI User Group and SQL Server User Group (JSSUG). His personal blog can be found at Devin Knight's website.

I must give thanks to God; without God in my life, I would not be as blessed as I am daily. Thanks for the amazing team of authors: Brian, Mitchell, and Manuel have put in time after hours away from their families to bring this great book together. To my wife, Erin, and three children, Collin, Justin, and Lana, who were all patient during nights that daddy had to spend writing. Finally, I would like to thank Dirk Kalinowski, the best chess boxing coach a rising star like myself could ask for. I know this will be the year that we earn the heavyweight world champion title.

Brian Knight is the owner and founder of Pragmatic Works, and is a serial entrepreneur, having also started up other companies. Brian is a contributing columnist at several technical magazines. He is the author of 16 technical books. Brian has spoken at conferences such as PASS Summit, SQL Connections, TechEd, SQLSaturdays, and Code Camps. He has received a number of awards from the State of Florida, from both the governor and press, including the Business Ambassador Award (governor) and Top CEO (Jacksonville Magazine). His blog can be found at Pragmatic Works website.

Thanks to everyone who made this book possible. As always, I owe a huge debt to my wife, Jenn, for putting up with my late nights, and to my children, Colton, Liam, Camille, and John, for being so patient with their tired dad who has always overextended himself. Finally, I would like to thank Shawn Trautman, my line dancing instructor. This will be the year that we complete the United Country Western Dance Council's goal of making line dancing a competitive sport worldwide.

Mitchell Pearson has worked for Pragmatic Works for six years as a Business Intelligence Consultant and Training Content manager. Mitchell has experience developing enterprise level BI Solutions using the full suite of products offered by Microsoft (SSRS, SSIS, SSAS, and Power BI). Mitchell is very active in the community presenting at local user groups, SQL Saturday events, PASS virtual chapters and giving free webinars for Pragmatic Works. Mitchell can also be found blogging at Mitchellsql website. Mitchell is also the president of the local Power BI User Group in Jacksonville, Florida. In his spare time Mitchell spends his time with his wife and three kids. For fun Mitchell enjoys playing table top games with friends.

I would like to thank God for the gifts and opportunities afforded me and most of all for sending his son Jesus Christ. I would like to thank my wife and children for their patience and support as I worked on this book. I would also like to thank Brian Knight for the opportunity to learn and grow in the field of Business Intelligence. Finally, I would like to thank Anthony Martin, Dustin Ryan, Bradley Schacht, Devin Knight, Jorge Segarra, and Bradley Ball, each one of these individuals have provided guidance and mentoring through the years and have had a profound impact on my career.

Manuel Quintana is a Training Content Manager at Pragmatic Works. Previously, he was a senior manager working in the hotel industry. He joined the Pragmatic Works team in 2014 with no knowledge in the Business Intelligence space, but now speaks at SQL Saturdays and SQL Server User Groups locally and virtually. He also teaches various BI technologies to many different Fortune 500 companies on behalf of Pragmatic Works. Since 2014, he has called Jacksonville home and before that Orlando, but he was born on the island of Puerto Rico and loves to go back and visit his family. When he isn't working on creating new content for Pragmatic Works, you can probably find him playing board games or watching competitive soccer matches.

Thank you to all my family and friends who support me in all of my endeavors. Special praise must be given to my wife for supporting me during late hours working and some weekends being dedicated to writing this book, without her I wouldn't be the person I am proud of being today. Also, I must say thank you to all my coworkers at Pragmatic Works; each one of them has mentored me in one way or another, and all my success can be traced back to them. I hope to make everyone mentioned here proud of what I have done and what I will achieve.

About the reviewer

Nick Lee is Business Intelligence Consultant and trainer for Pragmatic Works' training team. He comes from a customer service background and has an ample amount of experience in presenting and interacting with large Organizations. His focus at Pragmatic Works is creating Power BI content and delivering Power BI classes to our customers

Packt is searching for authors like you

If you're interested in becoming an author for Packt, please visit `authors.packtpub.com` and apply today. We have worked with thousands of developers and tech professionals, just like you, to help them share their insight with the global tech community. You can make a general application, apply for a specific hot topic that we are recruiting an author for, or submit your own idea.

Table of Contents

Preface

As an experienced BI professional, you may have, at one time, considered your skills irreplaceable. However, while you were tirelessly building the most elegant data warehouse solutions, Microsoft was busy building a new suite of self-service business intelligence and analytics tools called Power BI. Quickly, Power BI has become one of the most popular tools in the market, and users are looking to *you* for advice on how they should implement best practices and scale their own usage of the tool. While your corporate BI solutions will always be the gold standard for your company's enterprise data strategy, you can no longer ignore your company's hunger for self-server data wrangling.

In this book, you will learn how to bridge the gap of your existing corporate BI skillset into what's possible with Power BI. You will understand how to connect to data sources using both import and direct query options. You will then learn how to effectively use the Power BI Query Editor to perform transformations and data-cleansing processes to your data. This will include using R script and advanced M query transforms. Next, you will learn how to properly design your data model to navigate table relationships and use DAX formulas to enhance its usability. Visualizing your data is another key element of this book, as you will learn proper data visualization styles and enhanced digital storytelling techniques. Finally, by the end of this book, you will understand how to administer your company's Power BI environment so that deployment can be made seamless, data refreshes can run properly, and security can be fully implemented.

Who this book is for

This book is intended for business intelligence professionals who have experience with traditional enterprise BI tools in the past and now need a guide to jumpstart their knowledge of Power BI. Individuals new to business intelligence will also gain a lot from reading this book, but knowledge of some industry terminology will be assumed. Concepts covered in this book can also be helpful for BI managers beginning their companies' self-service BI implementation. Prior knowledge of Power BI is helpful but certainly not required for this book.

What this book covers

Chapter 1, *Getting Started with Importing Data*, begins by getting the audience oriented with the Power BI Desktop. Next, they will learn how to connect to various common data sources in Power BI. Once a data source is chosen, the options within will be explored, including the choice between data import, direct query, and live connection.

Chapter 2, *Data Transformation Strategies*, explores the capabilities of the Power Query Editor inside the Power BI Desktop. Using this Power BI Query Editor, the reader will first learn how to do basic transformations, and they will quickly learn more advanced data-cleansing practices. By the end of this chapter, the audience will know how to combine queries, use parameters, and read and write basic M queries.

Chapter 3, *Building the Data Model*, discusses one of the most critical parts of building a successful Power BI solution—designing an effective data model. In this chapter, readers will learn that while designing a data model, they are really setting themselves up for success when it comes to building reports. Specifically, this chapter will teach the audience how to establish relationships between tables, how to deal with complex relationship designs, and how to implement usability enhancements for the report consumers.

Chapter 4, *Leveraging DAX*, teaches that the Data Analysis Expression (DAX) language within Power BI is critical to building data models that are valuable to data consumers. While DAX may be intimidating at first, readers will quickly learn that its roots come from the Excel formula engine. This can be helpful at first, but as you find the need to develop more and more complex calculations, readers will learn that having a background in Excel formulas will only take them so far. This chapter will start with an understanding of basic DAX concepts but quickly accelerate into more complex ideas, such as like Time Intelligence and Filter Context.

Chapter 5, *Visualizing Data*, describes how to take a finely tuned data model and build reports that properly deliver a message that clearly and concisely tells a story about the data.

Chapter 6, *Digital Storytelling with Power BI*, covers the capability Power BI has to be much more than just a simple drag-and-drop reporting tool. Using the storytelling features of Drillthrough Filters, Bookmarks, and the Selection pane, you have the ability to design reports that not only display data but also tell engaging stories that make your users crave for more.

Chapter 7, *Using a Cloud Deployment with the Power BI Service*, examines deploying your solution to the Power BI Service to share what you've developed with your organization. Once deployed, you can build dashboards, share them with others, and schedule data refreshes. This chapter will cover the essential skills a BI professional would need to know to top off a Power BI solution they have developed.

Chapter 8, *On-Premises Solutions with Power BI Report Server*, explores how many organizations have decided that they are not yet ready to move to the cloud. Using the Power BI Report Server cloud, wary organizations get the benefit of Power BI reports without compromising their feelings about the cloud. This chapter will cover deploying to the Power BI Report Server cloud, sharing reports with others, and updating data.

To get the most out of this book

After downloading and installing the Power BI Desktop, you will be able to follow the majority of the examples in this book. By subscribing to the Power BI Pro license, you can follow all examples in this book. There are also supplementary files you can download to follow the book examples.

Download the example code files

You can download the example code files for this book from your account at www.packtpub.com. If you purchased this book elsewhere, you can visit www.packtpub.com/support and register to have the files emailed directly to you.

You can download the code files by following these steps:

1. Log in or register at www.packtpub.com.
2. Select the **SUPPORT** tab.
3. Click on **Code Downloads & Errata**.
4. Enter the name of the book in the **Search** box and follow the onscreen instructions.

Once the file is downloaded, please make sure that you unzip or extract the folder using the latest version of:

- WinRAR/7-Zip for Windows
- Zipeg/iZip/UnRarX for Mac
- 7-Zip/PeaZip for Linux

The code bundle for the book is also hosted on GitHub at `https://github.com/PacktPublishing/Microsoft-Power-BI-Quick-Start-Guide/`. In case there's an update to the code, it will be updated on the existing GitHub repository.

We also have other code bundles from our rich catalog of books and videos available at `https://github.com/PacktPublishing/`. Check them out!

Download the color images

We also provide a PDF file that has color images of the screenshots/diagrams used in this book. You can download it here: `http://www.packtpub.com/sites/default/files/downloads/Microsoft PowerBIQuickStartGuide_ColorImages.pdf`.

Conventions used

There are a number of text conventions used throughout this book.

`CodeInText`: Indicates code words in text, database table names, folder names, filenames, file extensions, pathnames, dummy URLs, user input, and Twitter handles. Here is an example: "Mount the downloaded `WebStorm-10*.dmg` disk image file as another disk in your system."

Bold: Indicates a new term, an important word, or words that you see onscreen. For example, words in menus or dialog boxes appear in the text like this. Here is an example: "Select **System info** from the **Administration** panel."

 Warnings or important notes appear like this.

 Tips and tricks appear like this.

Get in touch

Feedback from our readers is always welcome.

General feedback: Email `feedback@packtpub.com` and mention the book title in the subject of your message. If you have questions about any aspect of this book, please email us at `questions@packtpub.com`.

Errata: Although we have taken every care to ensure the accuracy of our content, mistakes do happen. If you have found a mistake in this book, we would be grateful if you would report this to us. Please visit `www.packtpub.com/submit-errata`, selecting your book, clicking on the Errata Submission Form link, and entering the details.

Piracy: If you come across any illegal copies of our works in any form on the Internet, we would be grateful if you would provide us with the location address or website name. Please contact us at `copyright@packtpub.com` with a link to the material.

If you are interested in becoming an author: If there is a topic that you have expertise in and you are interested in either writing or contributing to a book, please visit `authors.packtpub.com`.

Reviews

Please leave a review. Once you have read and used this book, why not leave a review on the site that you purchased it from? Potential readers can then see and use your unbiased opinion to make purchase decisions, we at Packt can understand what you think about our products, and our authors can see your feedback on their book. Thank you!

For more information about Packt, please visit `packtpub.com`.

Getting Started with Importing Data Options

1

Power BI may very well be one of the most aptly named tools ever developed by Microsoft, giving analysts and developers a powerful business intelligence and analytics playground while still packaging it in a surprisingly lightweight application. Using Microsoft Power BI, the processes of data discovery, data modeling, data visualization, and sharing are made elegantly simple using a single product. These processes are so commonplace when developing Power BI solutions that this book has adopted sections that follow this pattern. However, from your perspective, the really exciting thing may be that development problems that would previously take you weeks to solve in a corporate BI solution can now be accomplished in only hours.

Power BI is a **Software as a Service (SaaS)** offering in the Azure cloud, and, as such, the Microsoft product team follows a strategy of *cloud first* as they develop and add new features to the product. However, this does not mean that Power BI is only available in the cloud. Microsoft presents two options for sharing your results with others. The first, most often-utilized method is the cloud-hosted Power BI Service, which is available to users for a low monthly subscription fee. The second option is the on-premises Power BI Report Server, which can be obtained through either your SQL Server licensing with Software Assurance, or a subscription level known as Power BI Premium. Both solutions require a development tool called Power BI Desktop, which is available for free, and is where you must start to design your solutions.

Using the **Power BI Desktop** application enables you to define your data discovery and data preparation steps, organize your data model, and design engaging data visualizations on your reports. In this first chapter, the development environment will be introduced, and the data discovery process will be explored in depth. The topics detailed in this chapter include the following:

- Getting started
- Importing data
- Direct query
- Live Connection

Getting started

The Power BI Desktop is available free and can be found via a direct download link at Power BI(https://powerbi.microsoft.com/), or by installing it as an app from Windows Store. There are several benefits in using the Windows Store Power BI app, including automatic updates, no requirement for admin privileges, and making it easier for planned IT roll-out of Power BI.

 If you are using the on-premises Power BI Report Server for your deployment strategy, then you must download a different **Power BI Desktop**, which is available by clicking the advanced download options at https://powerbi.microsoft.com/en-us/report-server/. A separate install is required because updates are released more often to Power BI in the cloud. This book will be written primarily under the assumption that the reader is using the cloud-hosted Power BI Service as their deployment strategy.

Once you download, install, and launch the Power BI Desktop, you will likely be welcomed by the Start screen, which is designed to help new users find their way. Close this start screen so we can review some of the most commonly used features of the application:

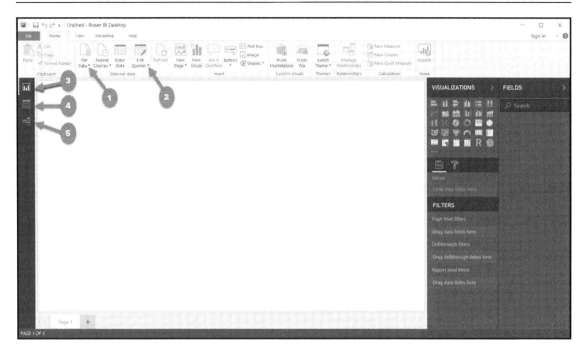

Power BI Deskstop

Following the numbered figures, let's learn the names and purposes of some of the most important features in the Power BI Desktop:

- **Get Data**: Used for selecting and configuring data sources.
- **Edit Queries**: Launches the **Power Query Editor**, which is used for applying data transformations to incoming data.
- **Report View**: The report canvas used for designing data visualizations. This is the default view open when the Power BI Desktop is launched.
- **Data View**: Provides a view of the data in your model. This looks similar to a typical Excel spreadsheet, but it is read-only.
- **Relationship View**: Primarily used when your data model has multiple tables and relationships need to be defined between them.

Importing data

Power BI is best known for the impressive data visualizations and dashboard capabilities it has. However, before you can begin building reports, you first need to connect to the necessary data sources. Within the Power BI Desktop, a developer has more than 80 unique data connectors to choose from, ranging from traditional file types, database engines, big data solutions, cloud sources, data stored on a web page, and other SaaS providers. This book will not cover all 80 connectors that are available, but it will highlight some of the most popular.

When establishing a connection to a data source, you may be presented with one of three different options on how your data should be treated: Import, DirectQuery, or Live Connection. This section will focus specifically on the Import option.

Choosing to import data, which is the most common option, and default behavior, means that Power BI will physically extract rows of data from the selected source and store it in an in-memory storage engine within Power BI. The Power BI Desktop uses a special method for storing data, known as xVelocity, which is an in-memory technology that not only increases the performance of your query results but can also highly compress the amount of space taken up by your Power BI solution. In *some* cases, the compression that takes place can even lower the disk space required up to one-tenth of the original data source size. The xVelocity engine uses a local unseen instance of **SQL Server Analysis Services (SSAS)** to provide these in-memory capabilities.

There are consequences to using the import option within Power BI that you should also consider. These consequences will be discussed later in this chapter, but as you read on, consider the following:

- How does data that has been imported into Power BI get updated?
- What if I need a dashboard to show near real-time analytics?
- How much data can really be imported into an in-memory storage system?

Excel as a source

Believe it or not, Excel continues to be the most popular application in the world and as such you should expect that at some point you will be using it as a data source:

1. To get started, open the Power BI Desktop and close the start-up screen if it automatically appears.

2. Under the **Home** ribbon, you will find that **Get Data** button, which you already learned is used for selecting and configuring data sources. Selecting the down arrow next to the button will show you the most common connectors, but selecting the center of the button will launch the full list of all available connectors. Regardless of which way you select the button, you will find Excel at the top of both lists.

3. Navigate to and open the file called `AdventureWorksDW.xlsx` from the book resources. This will launch the **Navigator** dialog, which is used for selecting the objects in the Excel workbook you desire to take data from:

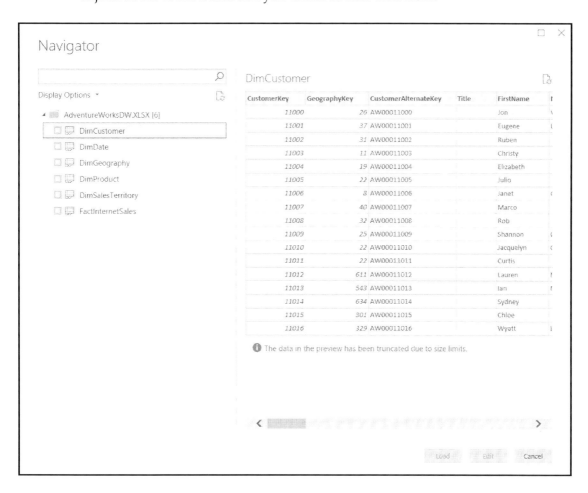

4. In this example, you see six separate spreadsheets you can choose from. Clicking once on the spreadsheet name will give you a preview of the data it stores, while clicking the checkbox next to the name will include it as part of the data import. For this example, select the checkboxes next to all of the available objects, then notice the options available in the bottom right.

5. Selecting **Load** will immediately take the data from the selected spreadsheets and import them as separate tables in your Power BI data model. Choosing **Edit** will launch an entirely new window called the **Power Query Editor** that allows you to apply business rules or transforms to your prior to importing it. You will learn much more about the **Power Query Editor** in Chapter 2, *Data Transformation Strategies*. Since you will learn more about this later, simply select **Load** to end this example.

Another topic you will learn more about in Chapter 7, *Using a Cloud Deployment with the Power BI Service*, is the concept of data refreshes. This is important because, when you import data into Power BI, that data remains static until another refresh is initiated. This refresh can either by initiated manually or set on a schedule. This also requires the installation of a Data Gateway, the application in charge of securely pushing data into the Power BI Service. Feel free to skip to Chapter 7, *Using a Cloud Deployment with the Power BI Service*, if configuring a data refresh is a subject you need to know now.

SQL Server as a source

Another common source designed for relational databases is Microsoft SQL Server:

1. To connect to SQL Server, select the **Get Data** button again, but this time choose **SQL Server**. Here, you must provide the server, but the database is optional and can be selected later:

2. For the first time, you are asked to choose the type of **Data Connectivity mode** you would like. As mentioned previously, **Import** is the default mode, but you can optionally select **DirectQuery**. DirectQuery will be discussed in greater detail later in this chapter. Expanding the **Advanced** options provides a way to insert a SQL statement that may be used as your source. For the following example, in the server is the only one property populated before clicking **OK**:

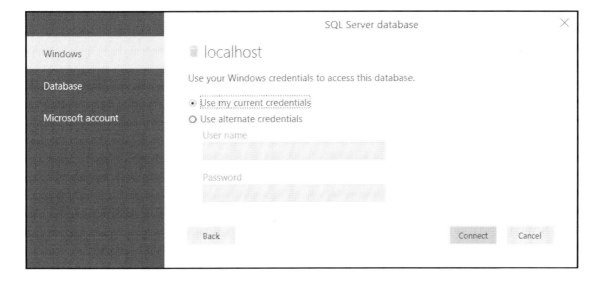

3. Next, you will be prompted to provide the credentials you are using to connect to the database server you provided on the previous screen.

4. Click **Connect** after providing the proper credentials to launch the same **Navigator** dialog that you may remember from when you connected to Excel. Here, you will select the tables, views, or functions within your SQL Server database that you desire to import into your Power BI solution. Once again, the final step in this dialog allows you to choose to either **Load** or **Edit** the results.

Web as a source

One pleasant surprise to many Power BI Developers is the availability of a web connector. Using this connection type allows you to source data from files that are stored on a website or even data that has been embedded into an HTML table on the web page. Using this type of connector can often be helpful when you would like to supplement your internal corporate data sources with information that can be publicly found on the internet.

For this example, imagine you are working for a major automobile manufacturer in the United States. You have already designed a Power BI solution using data internally available within your organization that shows historical patterns in sales trends. However, you would like to determine whether there are any correlations in periods of historically higher fuel prices and lower automobile sales. Fortunately, you found that the United States Department of Labor publicly posts historical average consumer prices of many commonly purchased items, including fuel prices.

1. Now that you understand the scenario within the Power BI Desktop, select the **Get Data** button and choose **Web** as your source. You will then be prompted to provide the URL where the data can be found. In this example, the data can be found by searching on the website Data.Gov (`https://www.data.gov/`) or, to save you some time, use the direct link: `https://download.bls.gov/pub/time.series/ap/ap.data.2.Gasoline`. Once you provide the URL, click **OK**:

2. Next, you will likely be prompted with an **Access Web Content** dialog box. This is important when you are using a data source that requires a login to access. Since this data source does not require a login to find the data, you can simply select anonymous access, which is the default, and then click **Connect**:

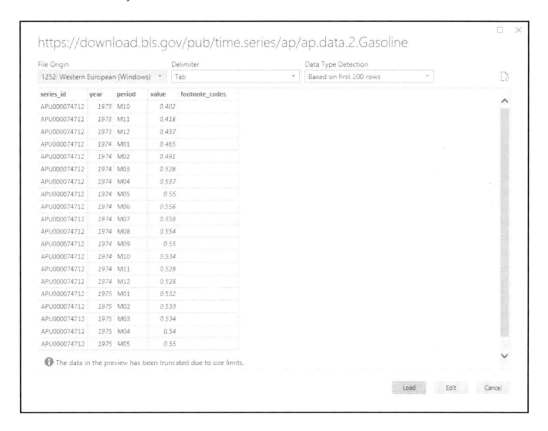

Notice on the next screen that the Power BI Desktop recognizes the URL provided as a tab-delimited file that can now easily be added to any existing data model you have designed.

DirectQuery

Many of you have likely been trying to envision how you may implement these data imports in your environment. You may ask yourself questions such as the following:

- If data imported into Power BI uses an in-memory technology, did my company provide me a machine that has enough memory to handle this?
- Am I really going to import my source table with tens of billions of rows into memory?
- How do I handle a requirement of displaying results in real time from the source?

These are all excellent questions that would have many negative answers if the only way to connect to your data was by importing your source into Power BI. Fortunately, there is another way. Using **DirectQuery**, Power BI allows you to connect directly to a data source so that no data is imported or copied into the Power BI Desktop.

Why is this a good thing? Consider the questions that were asked at the beginning of this section. Since no data is imported to the Power BI Desktop, that means it is less important how powerful your personal laptop is because all query results are now processed on the source server instead of your laptop. It also means that there is no need to refresh the results in Power BI because any reports you design are always pointing to a live version of the data source. That's a huge benefit!

Enabling this feature can be done by simply selecting **DirectQuery** during the configuration of a data source. The following screenshot shows a connection to an SQL Server database with the **DirectQuery** option selected:

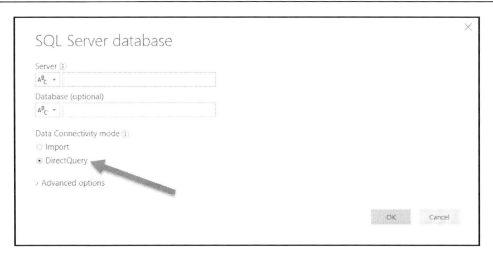

Earlier in this chapter, the Data Gateway application was mentioned as a requirement to schedule data refreshes for sources that used the import option. This same application is also needed with DirectQuery if your data is an on-premises source. Even though there is no scheduled data refresh, the Data Gateway is still required to push on-premises data into the cloud. Again, this will be discussed in more depth in `Chapter 7`, *Using a Cloud Deployment with the Power BI Service*.

Limitations

So, if DirectQuery is so great, why not choose it every time? Well, with every great feature you will also find limitations. The first glaring limitation is that not all data sources support DirectQuery. As of the time this book was written, the following data sources support DirectQuery in Power BI:

- Amazon Redshift
- Azure HDInsight Spark
- Azure SQL Database
- Azure SQL Data Warehouse
- Google BigQuery
- IBM Netezza
- Impala (Version 2.x)
- Oracle Database (Version 12 and above)
- SAP Business Warehouse Application Server

- SAP Business Warehouse Message Server
- SAP HANA
- Snowflake
- Spark (Version 0.9 and above)
- SQL Server
- Teradata Database
- Vertica

Depending on the data source you choose, there is a chance of slower query performance when using DirectQuery compared to the default data import option. Keep in mind that when the import option is selected it leverages a highly sophisticated in-memory storage engine. When selecting **DirectQuery**, performance will depend on the source type you have chosen from the list above.

Another limitation worth noting is that not all Power BI features are supported when you choose **DirectQuery**. For example, depending on the selected source, *some* the **Power Query Editor** features are disabled and could result in the following message: **This step results in a query that is not supported in DirectQuery mode**. Another example is that some DAX functions are unavailable when using DirectQuery. For instance, several Time Intelligence functions such as TotalYTD would generate the following type error when using DirectQuery:

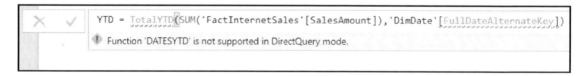

```
YTD = TotalYTD(SUM('FactInternetSales'[SalesAmount]),'DimDate'[FullDateAlternateKey])
```
Function 'DATESYTD' is not supported in DirectQuery mode.

The reason for this limitation is because DirectQuery automatically attempts to convert DAX functions such as this one to a query in the data source's native language. So, if the source of this solution was SQL Server, then Power BI would attempt to convert this DAX function into a comparable T-SQL script. Once Power BI realizes the DAX function used is not compatible with the source, the error is generated.

You can turn on functions that DirectQuery blocks by going to **File** | **Options and settings** | **Options** | **DirectQuery** | **Allow unstricted measures in DirectQuery Mode**. When this option is selected, any DAX expressions that are valid for a measure can be used. However, you should know that selecting this can result in very slow query performance when these blocked functions are used.

Live Connection

The basic concept of Live Connection is very similar to that of DirectQuery. Just like DirectQuery, when you use a Live Connection no data is actually imported into Power BI. Instead, your solution points directly to the underlying data source and leverages Power BI Desktop simply as a data visualization tool. So, if these two things are so similar, then why give them different names? The answer is because even though the basic concept is the same, DirectQuery and Live Connection vary greatly.

One difference that should quickly be noticeable is the query performance experience. It was mentioned in the last section that DirectQuery can often have poor performance depending on the data source type. With Live Connection, you generally will not have any performance problem because it is only supported by the following types of data sources:

- SQL Server Analysis Services Tabular
- SQL Server Analysis Services Multidimensional
- Power BI Service

The reason performance does not suffer with these data sources is because they either use the same xVelocity engine that Power BI does, or another high-performance storage engine. To set up your own Live Connection to one of these sources, you can choose the **SQL Server Analysis Services** database from the list of sources after selecting **Get Data**. Here, you can specify that the connection should be live:

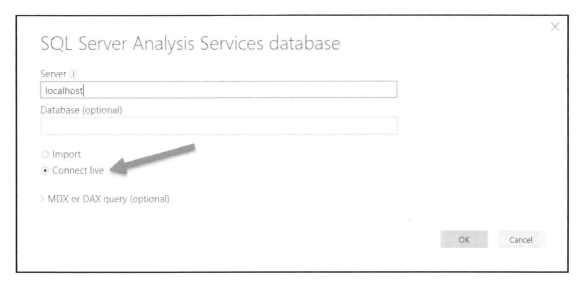

If a dataset is configured for a Live Connection or DirectQuery, then you can expect automatic refreshes to occur approximately each hour or when interaction with the data occurs. You can manually adjust the refresh frequency in the Scheduled cache refresh option in the Power BI service.

Limitations

So far, this sounds great! You have now learned that you can connect directly to your data sources, without importing data into your model, and you won't have significant performance consequences. Of course, these benefits don't come without giving something up, so what are the limitations of a Live Connection?

What you will encounter with Live Connections are limitations that are generally a result of the fact that Analysis Services is an Enterprise BI tool. Thus, if you are going to connect to it, then it has probably already gone through significant data cleansing and modeling by your IT team.

Modeling capabilities such as defining relationships are not available because these would be designed in an Analysis Services Model. Also, the Power Query Editor is not available at all against a Live Connection source. While at times this may be frustrating, it does make sense that it works this way because any of the changes you may desire to make with relationships or in the query editor should be done in Analysis Services, not Power BI.

Which should I choose?

Now that you have learned about the three different ways to connect to your data, you're left to wonder which option is best for you. It's fair to say that the choice you make will really depend on the requirements of each individual project you have. To summarize, some of the considerations that were mentioned in this chapter are listed in the following table:

Consideration	Import Data	DirectQuery	Live Connection
Best performance	X		X
Best design experience	X		
Best for keeping data up-to-date		X	X
Data sources availability	X		
Most scalable		X	X

Some of these items to consider may be more important than others to you. So, to make this more personal, try using the Decision Matrix file that is included with this book. In this file, you can rank (from 1 to 10) the importance of each of these considerations to help give you some guidance on which option is best for you.

Since the Data Import option presents the most available features, going forward, this book primarily uses this option. In `Chapter 2`, *Data Transformation Strategies*, you will learn how to implement data transformation strategies to ensure all the necessary business rules are applied to your data.

Summary

Power BI provides users a variety of methods for connecting to data sources with natively built-in data connectors. The connector you choose for your solution will depend on where your data is located. Once you connect to a data source, you can decide on what type of query mode best suits your needs. Some connectors allow for zero latency in your results with the options of Direct Query or Live Connection. In this chapter, you learned about the benefits and disadvantages of each query mode, and you were given a method for weighting these options using a decision matrix. In the next chapter, you will learn more about how data transformations may be applied to your data import process so that incoming data will be properly cleansed.

Data Transformation Strategies

2

Within any BI project, it is essential that the data you are working with has been properly scrubbed to make for accurate results on your reports and dashboards. Applying data cleansing business rules, also known as transforms, is the method for correcting inaccurate or malformed data, but the process can often be the most time-consuming part of any corporate BI solution. However, the data transformation capabilities built into Power BI are both very powerful and user-friendly. Using the Power Query Editor, tasks that would typically be difficult or time-consuming in an enterprise BI tool are as simple as right-clicking on a column and selecting the appropriate transform for the field. While interacting with the user interface in this editor, a language called M is being written automatically for you behind the scenes.

Through the course of this chapter, you will explore some of the most common features of the Power Query Editor that make it so highly regarded by its users. Since one sample dataset cannot provide all the problems you will run into, you will be provided several small disparate examples to show you what is possible. This chapter will detail the following topics:

- The Power Query Editor
- Transform basics
- Advanced data transformation options
- Leveraging R
- M formula language

The Power Query Editor

The **Power Query Editor** is the primary tool that you will utilize for applying data transformations and cleansing processes to your solution. This editor can be launched as part of establishing a connection to your data, or by simply clicking **Edit Queries** on the **Home** ribbon of the Power BI Desktop. When the Power Query editor is opened, you will notice that it has its own separate environment for you to work in. The environment encapsulates a user-friendly method for working with all of the queries that you will define. Before you dive deep into the capabilities of the Power Query Editor, let's first start by doing an overview of the key areas that are most important:

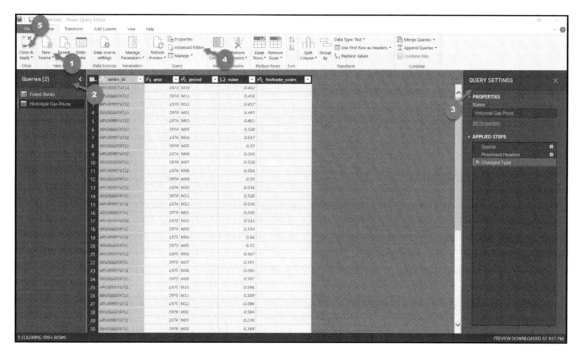

Power BI Deskstop

Following the numbered figures, let's review some of the most important features of the Power Query Editor:

- **New Source**: This launches the same interface as the **Get Data** button that you learned about in `Chapter 1`, *Getting Started with Importing Data Options*.
- **Queries Pane**: A list of all the queries that you have connected to. From here, you can rename a query, disable the load and refresh capabilities, and organize your queries into groups.

- **Query Settings**: Within this pane, you can rename the query, but more importantly you can see and change the list of steps, or transforms, that have been applied to your query.
- **Advanced Editor**: By launching the **Advanced Editor**, you can see the M query that is automatically written for you by the Power Query Editor.
- **Close & Apply**: Choosing this option will close the **Power Query Editor** and load the results into the data model.

Transform basics

Applying data transformations within the **Power Query Editor** can be a surprisingly simple thing to do. However, there are few things to consider as we begin this process. The first is that there are multiple ways to solve a problem. As you work your way through this book, the authors have tried to show you the fastest and easiest methods of solving the problems that are presented, but these solutions certainly will not be the only ways to reach your goals.

The next thing you should understand is that every click you do inside the **Power Query Editor** is automatically converted into a formula language called M. Virtually all the basic transforms you will ever need can be accomplished by simply interacting with the **Power Query Editor** user interface, but for more complex business problems there is a good chance you may have to at least modify the M queries that are written for you by the editor. You will learn more about M later in this chapter.

Finally, the last important consideration to understand is that all transforms that are created within the editor are stored in the **Query Settings** pane under a section called **Applied Steps**. Why is this important to know? The **Applied Steps** section has many features, but here are some of the most critical to know for now:

- **Deleting transforms**: If you make a mistake and need to undo a step, you can click the **Delete** button next to a step.
- **Modifying transforms**: This can be done with any step that has a gear icon next to it.
- **Changing the order of transforms**: If you realize that it is better for one step to execute before another one, you can change the order of how the steps are executed.
- Clicking on any step prior to the current one will allow you to see how your query results would earlier in the process.

With this understanding, you will now get hand-on with applying several basic transforms inside the Power Query Editor. The goal of these first sets of example is to get you comfortable with the Power Query user interface before the more complex use cases are covered.

Use First Row as Headers

Organizing column names or headers is often an important first task when organizing your dataset. Providing relevant column names makes many of the downstream processes, such as building reports, much easier. Often, column headers are automatically imported from your data source, but sometimes you may be working with more unique data source that make it difficult for Power BI to capture the column header information. This walkthrough will show how to deal with such a scenario:

1. Launch the Power BI Desktop, and click **Get Data** under the **Home** ribbon.
2. Choose **Excel**, then navigate and select Open on the Failed Bank List.xlsx file that is available in the book source files.
3. In the **Navigator** window, select the table called Data, then choose **Edit**. When the **Power Query Editor** launches, you should notice that the column headers are not automatically imported. In fact, the column headers are in the first row of the data.
4. To push the column names that are in the first row of data to the header section, select the transform called **Use First Row as Headers** from the **Home** ribbon:

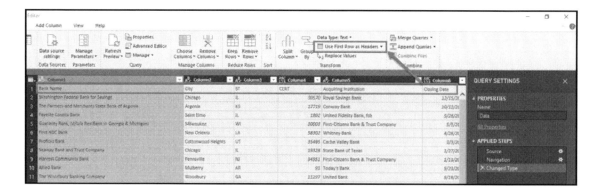

Remove Columns

Often, the data sources you will connect to will include many columns that are not necessary for the solution you are designing. It is important to remove these unnecessary columns from your dataset because these unused columns needlessly take up space inside your data model. There are several different methods for removing columns in the Power Query Editor. This example will show one of these methods using the same dataset from the prior demonstration:

1. Multi-select (*Ctrl* + click) the column headers of the columns you wish to keep as part of your solution. In this scenario, select the columns **Bank Name**, **City**, **ST**, and **Closing Date**.
2. With these four columns selected, right-click on any of the selected columns and choose **Remove Other Columns**. Once this transform is completed, you should be left with only the columns you need:

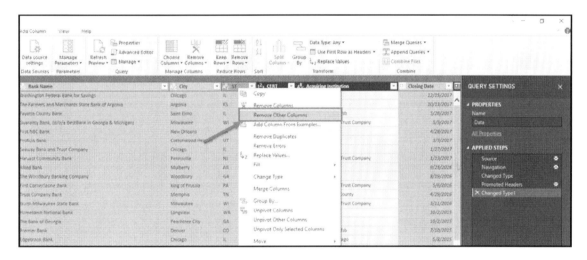

Option to Remove Other Columns

Another popular method for removing columns is clicking the **Choose Columns** button on the **Home** ribbon of the **Power Query Editor**. This option provides a list of all the columns, and you can choose the columns you wish to keep or exclude.

You can also select the columns you wish to remove; right-click on one of the selected columns and click Remove. This seems like the more obvious method. However, this option is not as user-friendly in the long run because it does not provide an option to edit the transform in the **Applied Steps** section like the first two methods allow.

Change type

Defining column data types properly early on in your data scrubbing process can help to determine the type of values you are working with. The **Power Query Editor** has various numeric, text, and date-time data types for you to choose from. In our current example, all of the data types were automatically interpreted correctly by the **Power Query Editor**, but let's look at where you could change this if necessary:

1. Locate the data type indicator on the column header to the right of the column name
2. Click the data type icon, and a menu will open that allows you to choose the new data type you desire:

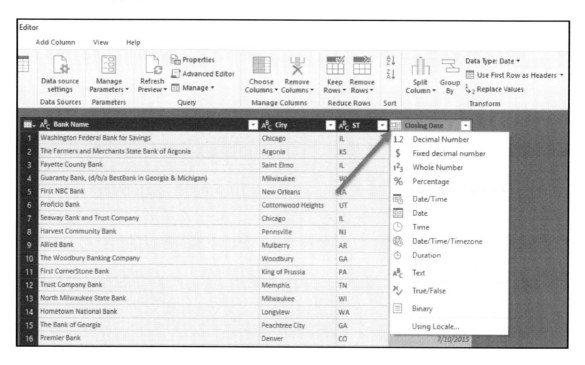

Choosing the Data type

Another method you can use for changing column data types is to right-click on the column you wish to change, then select Change Type and choose the new data type you desire.

If you want to change multiple column data types at once, you can multi-select the necessary columns, then select the new data type from the Data Type property under the **Home** ribbon.

Many of the transforms you will encounter in the future are contextually based on the column data types you are working with. For example, if you have a column that is a date then you will be provided special transforms that can only be executed against a date data type, such as extracting the month name from a date column.

Add Column From Examples

One option that can make complex data transformations seem simple is the feature called Add Column From Examples. Using Add Column From Examples, you can provide the Power Query Editor a sample of what you would like your data to look like, and it can then automatically determine which transforms are required to accomplish your goal. Continuing with the same failed banks example, let's walk through a simple example of how to use this feature:

1. Find and select the **Add Column** tab in the Power Query Editor ribbon.
2. Select the **Column From Example** button and, if prompted, choose **From All Columns**. This will launch a new **Add Column From Examples** interface.
3. Our goal is to leverage this feature to combine the `City` and `ST` columns together. In the first empty cell, `type Chicago, IL` and then hit Enter. You should notice that below the text you typed Power BI has automatically translated what you typed into a transform that can be applied for every row in the dataset.

4. Once you click **OK**, the transform is finalized and automatically added to the overall M query that has been built through the user interface:

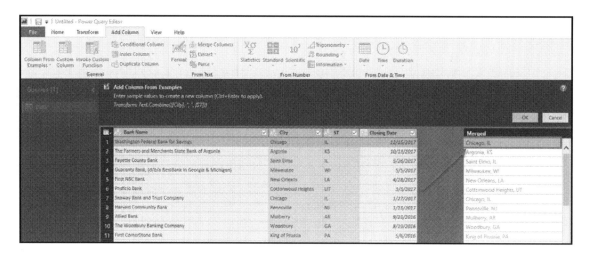

Adding Columns from Examples

Sometimes, you may encounter scenarios where the **Add Column From Examples** feature needs more than one example to properly translate your example into an M query function that accomplishes your goal. If this happens, simply provide additional examples of how you would like the data to appear, and the **Power Query Editor** should adjust to account for outliers.

Advanced data transformation options

Now that you should be more comfortable working within the Power Query Editor, let's take the next step in working with it. Often, you will find the need to go beyond these basic transforms when dealing with data that requires more care. In this section, you will learn about some of the more common advanced transforms that you may have a need for, which include Conditional Columns, Fill down, Unpivot, Merge Queries, and Append Queries.

Conditional Columns

Using the **Power Query Conditional Columns** functionality is a great way to add new columns to your query that follow logical if/then/else statements. This concept of if/then/else is common across many programming languages, including Excel formulas. Let's review a real-world scenario where you would be required to do some data cleansing on a file before it can be used. In this example, you will be provided a file of all the counties in the United States, and you must create a new column that extracts the state name from the county column and places it in its own column:

1. Start by connecting to the FIPS_CountyName.txt file that is found in the book files using the Text/CSV connector.
2. Launch the **Power Query Editor**, and start by changing the data type of Column1 to Text. When you do this, you will be prompted to replace an existing type conversion. You can accept this by clicking **Replace current**.
3. Now, on Column2, filter out **United States** from the field to remove this value from the column.
4. Remove the **state abbreviation** from Column2 by right-clicking on the column header and selecting **Split Column | By Delimiter**. Choose **-- Custom --** for the delimiter type, and type , , then click **OK**:

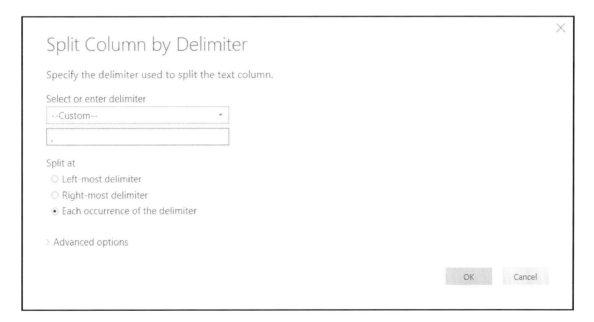

5. Next, rename the column names `Column1`, `Column2.1`, and `Column 2.2`, to `County Code`, `County Name`, and `State Abbreviation`, respectively.

6. To isolate the full state name into its own column, you will need to implement a **Conditional Column**. Go to the **Add Column** button in the ribbon and select **Conditional Column**.

7. Change the New column name property to `State Name` and implement the logic *If State Abbreviation equals null Then return County Name Else return null* as shown in the following screenshot. To return the value from another column, you must select the icon below the **text Output**, then choose **Select a column**. Once this is complete, click **OK**:

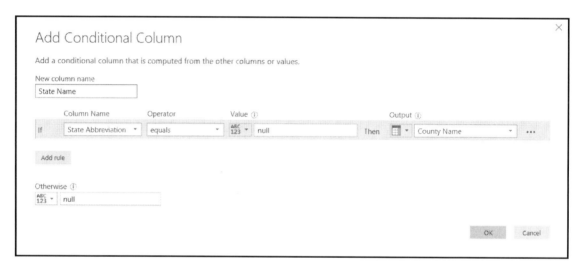

This results in a new column called `State Name`, which has the fully spelled-out state name only appearing on rows where the `State Abbreviation` is `null`.

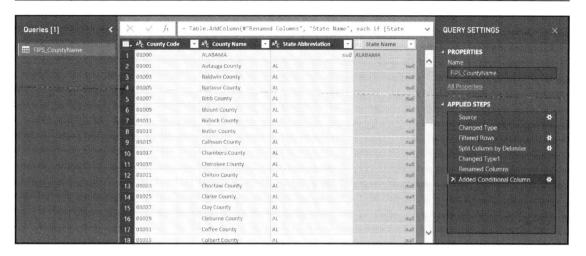

This is only setting the stage to fully scrub this dataset. To complete the data cleansing process for this file, read on to the next section. However, for the purposes of this example, you have now learned how to leverage the capabilities of the Conditional Column transform in the **Power Query Editor**.

Fill Down

Fill Down is a rather unique transform in how it operates. By selecting Fill Down on a particular column, a value will replace all Null values below it until another non-null appears. When another non-null value is present, that value will then fill down to all Null values. To examine this transform, you will pick up from where you left off with the Conditional Column example in the previous section.

1. Right-click on the **State Name** column header and select **Transform | | Capitalize Each Word**. This transform should be self-explanatory.
2. Next, select the State Name column and, in the Transform ribbon, select **Fill | | Down**. This will take the value in the State Name column and replace all non-null values until there is another State Name value that it can switch to. After preforming this transform, scroll through the results to ensure that the value of Alabama switches to Alaska when appropriate.

3. To finish this example, filter out any Null values that appear in the State Abbreviation column. The final result should look like this:

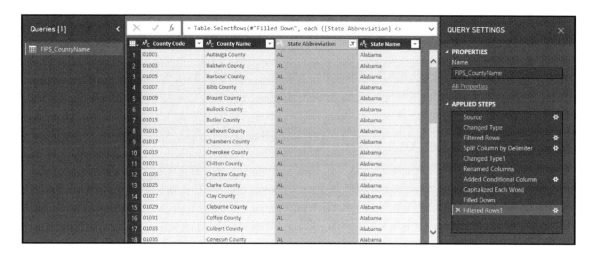

In this example, you learned how you can use **Fill Down** to replace all of the `null` values below a `non-null` value. You can also use **Fill Up** to do the opposite, which would replace all the `null` values above a `non-null` value.

Unpivot

The Unpivot transform is an incredibly powerful transform that allows you to reorganize your dataset into a more structured format for Business Intelligence. Let's discuss this by visualizing a practical example to help understand the purpose of Unpivot. Imagine you are provided a file that has the last three years of population by US States, and looks like this:

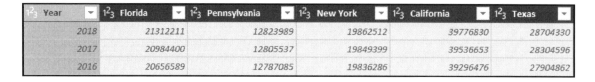

Year	Florida	Pennsylvania	New York	California	Texas
2018	21312211	12823989	19862512	39776830	28704330
2017	20984400	12805537	19849399	39536653	28304596
2016	20656589	12787085	19836286	39296476	27904862

The problem with data stored like this is you cannot very easily answer simple questions. For example, how would you answer questions like, *What was the total population for all states in the US in 2018* or *What was the average state population in 2016?* With the data stored in this format, simple reports are made rather difficult to design. This is where the Unpivot transform can be a lifesaver. Using Unpivot, you can change this dataset into something more acceptable for a BI project, like this:

Data stored in this format can now easily answer the questions posed earlier. To accomplish this in other programming languages can often require fairly complex logic, while the **Power Query Editor** does it in just a few clicks.

There are three different methods for selecting the Unpivot transform that you should be aware of, and include the following options:

- **Unpivot Columns**: Turns any selected columns headers into row values and the data in those columns into a corresponding row. With this selection, any new columns that may get added to the data source *will* automatically be included in the Unpivot transform.

- **Unpivot Other Columns**: Turns all column headers that *are not* selected into row values and the data in those columns into a corresponding row. With this selection, any new columns that may get added to the data source *will* automatically be included in the Unpivot transform.
- **Unpivot Only Selected Columns**: Turns any selected columns headers into row values and the data in those columns into a corresponding row. With this selection, any new columns that may get added to the data source *will not* be included in the Unpivot transform.

Let's walk through two examples of using the Unpivot transform to show you a few of these methods, and provide an understanding of how this complex problem can be solved with little effort in Power BI.

1. Launch a new instance of the Power BI Desktop, and use the Excel connector to import the workbook called `Income Per Person.xlsx` found in the book source files. Once you select this workbook, choose the spreadsheet called `Data` in the **Navigator** window, and then select **Edit** to launch the **Power Query Editor**.
2. Now, make the first row of data column headers by selecting the transform called **Use First Row as Headers** under the **Home** Ribbon.
3. Rename the column `GDP per capita PPP, with projections` column to `Country`.
4. If you look closely at the column headers, you can tell that most of the column names are actually years and the values inside those columns are the income for those years. This is not the ideal way to store this data because it would be incredibly difficult to answer the the question, *What is the average income per person for Belgium?* To make it easier to answer this type of question, right-click on the Country column and select **Unpivot Other Columns**.
5. Rename the `columns` Attribute and `Value to Year and Income,` respectively.

6. To finish this first example, you should also rename this query Income.

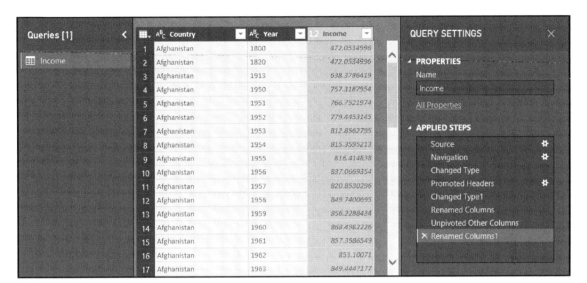

This first method walked you through what can often be the fastest method for performing an Unpivot transform, which is by using the Unpivot Other Columns option. In this next example, you will learn how to use the Unpivot Columns method.

1. Remain in the Power Query Editor, and select New Source from the Home Ribbon to use the Excel connector to import the workbook called Total Population.xlsx found in the book source files. Once you select this workbook, choose the spreadsheet called Data in the Navigator window, and then select OK.

2. Like the last example, you will again need to make the first row of data column headers by selecting the transform called Use First Row as Headers under the Home Ribbon.

3. Then, rename the column Total population to Country.

4. This time, multi-select all the columns except Country, then right-click on one of the selected columns and choose Unpivot Columns. The easiest way to multi-select these columns is to select the first column then hold *Shift* before clicking the last column.

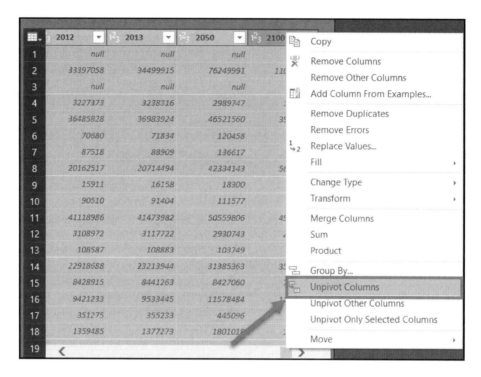

5. Rename the columns Attribute and Value to Year and Population, respectively.
6. To finish this first example, you should also rename this query Population.

In this section, you learned about two different methods for performing an Unpivot. To complete the data cleansing process on these two datasets, it's recommended that you continue through the next section on Merging Queries.

Merging Queries

A common requirement when building BI solutions is the need to join two tables together to form a new result that includes some columns from both tables in a single query. Fortunately, Power BI makes this task very simple with the **Merge Queries** feature. Using this feature requires that you select two tables and then determine which column or columns will be the basis of how the two queries are merged. After determining the appropriate columns for your join, you will select a join type. The join types are listed here with the description that is provided within the product.

- Left Outer (all from first, matching from second)
- Right Outer (all from second, matching from first)
- Full Outer (all rows from both)
- Inner (only matching rows)
- Left Anti (rows only in first)
- Right Anti (rows only in second)

Many of you may already be very familiar with these different join terms from SQL programming you have learned in the past. However, if these terms are all new to you I recommend reviewing Visualizing Merge Join Types in Power BI, courtesy of Jason Thomas in the Power BI Data Story Gallery: `https://community.powerbi.com/t5/Data-Stories-Gallery/Visualizing-Merge-Join-Types-in-Power-BI/m-p/219906`. This visual aid is a favorite of many users that are new to these concepts.

To examine the **Merge Queries** option, you will pick up from where you left off with the Unpivot examples in the previous section.

1. With the **Population query** selected, find and select **Merge Queries | Merge Queries as New** under the **Home** Ribbon.
2. In the **Merge dialog box**, select the **Income query** from the dropdown selection in the middle of the screen.
3. Then, multi-select the **Country** and **Year** columns under the **Population query**, and do the same under the **Income query**. This defines which columns will be used to join the two queries together. Ensure that the number indicators next to the column headers match. If they don't, you could accidentally attempt to join on the incorrect columns.

4. Next, select **Inner (only matching rows)** for the Join Kind. This join type will return rows only when the columns you chose to join on exist in both queries. Before you click **OK**, confirm that your screen looks like this:

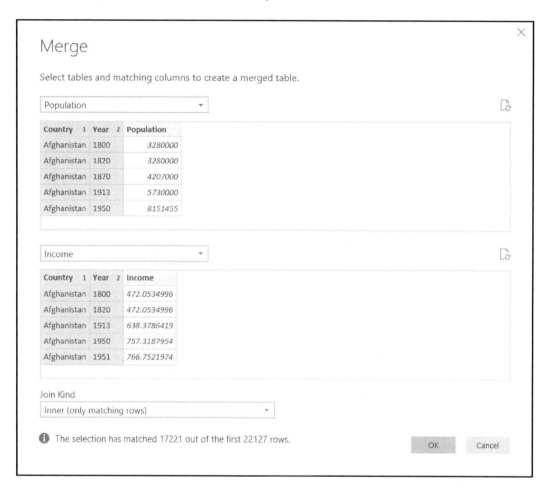

5. Once you select **OK**, this will create a new query called Merge1 that combines the results of the two queries. Go ahead and rename this query **Country Stats**.
6. You will also notice that there is a column called Income that has a value of Table for each row. This column is actually representative for the entire Income query that you joined to. To choose which columns you want from this query, click the **Expand** button on the column header. After clicking the **Expand** button, uncheck Country, Year, and Use original column name as prefix then click **OK**.

7. Rename the column called `Income.1` to `Income`.

8. Finally, since you chose the option `Merge Queries` as New in Step 1, you can disable the load option for the original queries that you started with. To do this, right-click on the `Income` query in the **Queries** pane and click **Enable Load** to disable it. Do the same thing for the **Population** query. Disabling these queries means that the only query that will be loaded into your Power BI data model is the new one, called **Country Stats**:

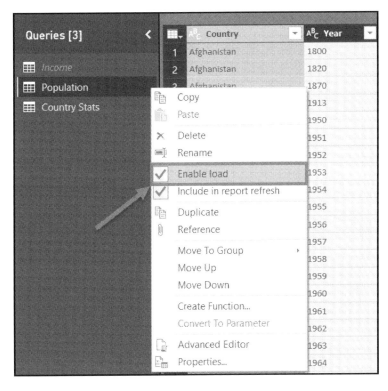

To begin using this dataset in a report, you would click Close & Apply. You will learn more about building reports in `Chapter 5`.

In this section, you learned how the **Merge Queries** option is ideal for joining two queries together. In the next section, you will learn how you could solve the problem of performing a union of two or more queries.

Appending Queries

Occasionally, you will work with multiple datasets that need to be appended to each other. Here's a scenario: you work for a customer service department for a company that provides credit to customers. You are regularly provided `.csv` and `.xlsx` files that give summaries of customer complaints regarding credit cards and student loans. You would like to be able to analyze both of these data extracts at the same time but, unfortunately, the credit card and student loan complaints are provided in two separate files. In this example, you will learn how to solve this problem by performing an append operation on these two different files.

1. Launch a new instance of the Power BI Desktop, and use the **Excel** connector to import the workbook called Student Loan `Complaints.xlsx` found in the book source files. Once you select this workbook, choose the spreadsheet called Student Loan Complaints in the Navigator window, and then select **Edit** to launch the Power Query Editor.

2. Next, import the credit card data by selecting **New Source | Text/CSV**, then choose the file called `Credit Card Complaints.csv` found in the book source files. Click **OK** to bring this data into the **Power Query Editor**.

3. With the **Credit Card Complaints** query selected, find and select **Append Queries | Append Queries as New** under the **Home** Ribbon.

4. Select **Student Loan Complaints** as the table to append to, then select **OK**.

5. Rename the newly created query **All Complaints**.

6. Similar to the previous example, you would likely want to disable the load option for the original queries that you started with. To do this, right-click on the Student **Load Complaints query** in the **Queries** pane, and click **Enable Load** to disable it.

7. Do the same to the **Credit Card Complaints** query, and then select **Close & Apply**.

Leveraging R

R is a very powerful scripting language that is primarily used for advanced analytics tools, but also has several integration points within Power BI. One such integration is the ability to apply business rules to your data with the R language. Why is that important? Well, with this capability you can extend beyond the limits of the Power Query Editor and call functions and libraries from R to do things that would not regularly be possible. In the next two sections, you will explore how to set up your machine to leverage R within Power BI and then walk through an example of using an R Script transform.

 There are many additional books and references you can read to learn more about the R scripting language, but for the purposes of this book, our goal is to inform you on what is possible when R and Power BI are combined.

Installation and configuration

To use R within Power BI, you must first install an R distribution for you to run and execute scripts against. In this book, we will leverage Microsoft's distribution, Microsoft R Open. It is an open source project and free for anyone to use. Once Microsoft R Open has been installed, you can then configure Power BI to recognize the home directory where R libraries may be installed. Let's walk through these setup steps together:

1. Navigate to the website `https://mran.microsoft.com/download/` to download and install Microsoft R Open.
2. For the purposes of our example, you will select **Download next to Microsoft R Open for Windows**.
3. Once the download has completed, run the installation and accept all default settings and user agreements.
4. Next, launch a new instance of the Power BI Desktop to set up the R integration with Power BI. Click the menu options **File** | **Options and settings** | **Options**.

5. Choose the R scripting section and ensure that the Detected R home directories property is filled with the R instance you just installed:

6. Once this is completed, click OK to begin using the capabilities of R within Power BI.

The R Script transform

With the R distribution now installed and configured to integrate with Power BI, you are now ready to see what's possible with these new capabilities. In this example, you will be looking at data from the European Stock Market. The problem with this dataset, that must be corrected with R, is that the file provided to you is missing values for certain days. So, to get a more accurate reading of the stock market, you will use an R package called MICE to impute the missing values:

1. Before beginning in Power BI you should ensure that the MICE library is installed and available in the R Distribute you installed in the last section. To do this, launch Microsoft R Open from your device. This is the basic RGui that was installed for you to run R scripts with.

    For many developers, the preferred method for writing R scripts is a free open source tool called RStudio. RStudio includes a code editor, debugging, and visualization tools that many find easier to work with. You can download RStudent from https://www.rstudio.com/.

2. Type the following script in the **R Console** window, and then hit *Enter*:

   ```
   install.packages("mice")
   ```

3. You can close the **R Console** and return to the Power BI Desktop after it returns back `package 'mice' successfully unpacked and MD5 sums checked`.

4. In the Power BI Desktop, start by connecting to the required csv data source called `EuStockMarkets_NA.csv` from the book source files. Once you connect to the file, click **Edit** to launch the **Power Query Editor**.

5. You will notice that there are a few days that are missing a **SMI (Stock Market Index)** value. The values that show NA we would like to replace using an R script. Go under the **Transform** ribbon, and select the **Run R Script** button on the far right.

6. Use the following R script to call the MICE library that you recently installed to detect what the missing values in this dataset should be:

   ```
   # 'dataset' holds the input data for this script
   library(mice)
   tempData <- mice(dataset,m=1,maxit=50,meth='pmm',seed=100)
   completedData <- complete(tempData,1)
   output <- dataset
   output$completedValues <- completedData$"SMI missing values"
   ```

7. Click **OK**, and then click on the hyperlink for table next to the **completedData** row to see the result of the newly implemented transform for detecting missing values.

This new output has replaced the missing values with new values that were detected based on the algorithm used within the R script. To now build a set of report visuals on this example, you can click **Close & Apply** under the **Home** ribbon.

This is just one simple way that R can be used with Power BI. You should note that in addition to using R as a transform, it can also be used as a data source and as a visual within Power BI.

M formula language

The **Power Query Editor** is the user interface that you have now learned is used to design and build data imports. However, you should also know that every transform you apply within this editor is actually, quietly and behind the scenes, writing an M query for you. The letter M here is a reference to the languages data mashup capabilities.

For simple solutions, it is unlikely that you will ever need to even look at the M query that is being written, but there are some more complex cases where it's helpful to understand how to read and write your own M. For the purposes of this book, covering just the Power BI essentials, you will learn how to find the M query editor within your solution and then understand how to read what it is doing for you. For the purposes of this example, you can open up any previously built example, however the screenshot used here is coming from the very first example in this chapter on basic transforms.

1. Using any Power BI solution you have designed, launch the **Power Query Editor**.
2. Under the **Home** Ribbon, select **Advanced Editor** to see the M query that has been written by the user interface:

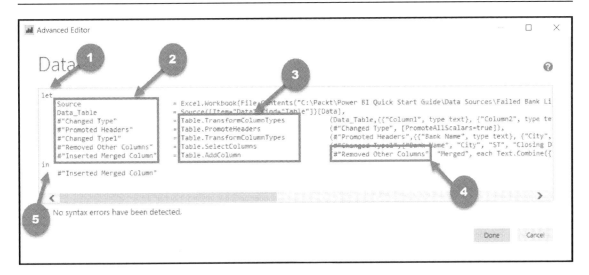

This query has been formatted to make it easier to read. Let's review the key elements that are present here:

1. **Let Expression**: Encapsulates a set of values or named expressions to be computed.
2. **Named Expressions or Variables**: The name given to a set of operations in a step. These names can be anything, but you should note that if you wish to have a space in the name of a step then it must be surrounded by #"". For example, If I wanted something to be called Step 1, then I would have to name an expression #"Step 1".
3. **M Functions**: The operations that are used to manipulate the data source.
4. **Prior Step Reference**: The M Query language generally executes its functions as serial operations, meaning each operation is executed one after the other sequentially. You can see this when you look at a query because each call to an M function always references the prior-named expression, to pick up where it left off.
5. **In Expression**: Oddly, the In expression is actually a reference to what the query will output. Whichever name expression is referenced in the In expression will be what is returned back in the Power Query Editor preview.

It is important to realize that M is case-sensitive. That means if you ever make a change to a query or write one from scratch, you should be careful because there is a difference between "a" and "A".

#shared

As mentioned previously, this book will not dive deep into writing your own M queries since that would be far beyond the essentials of Power BI. However, there is a great method for exploring the M functions that are available, and how to use them. Within the **Power Query editor**, you can use the #shared function to return back documentation on every available function in the M library. Let's walk through how you can leverage this tool:

1. In a new instance of the Power BI Desktop, select **Get Data** and then choose **Blank Query**. This will launch the **Power Query Editor** with an empty formula bar waiting for you to provide your own M.

2. In this formula bar, type = #shared, then hit *Enter*. Remember that M is case-sensitive so you must use a lower case "s" when typing "shared".

3. This will return a list of all the available M functions. By selecting the cell that has the hyperlink text of function, you can see documentation on how to use each function:

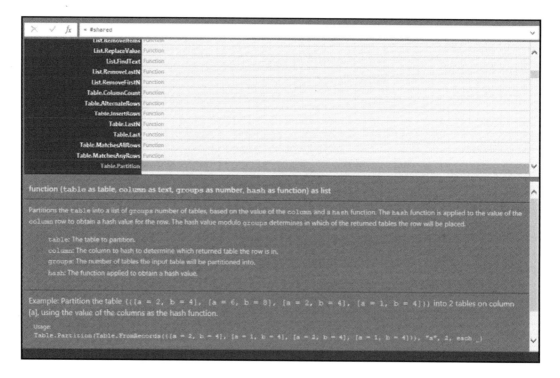

This is a great method for learning what M functions are available, and how each may be used.

Summary

In this chapter, you learned that the Power Query Editor is an extremely powerful tool for applying business rules to incoming data. Implementing data cleansing techniques can be as simple as right-clicking on a column, or more complex such as when building a Conditional Column. While the Power Query Editor does have a vast library of transforms available, you also learned that you can tap into the capabilities of R to extend what's possible when designing queries. Finally, this chapter also helped you learn that the decisions you make while building your queries can impact Query Folding, which can be incredibly important for the performance of your queries.

Building the Data Model 3

In this chapter, you are now going to create a coherent and intelligent data model by creating the necessary relationships to bring those data sources together. The topics detailed in this chapter are as follows:

- Building relationships
- Working with complex relationships
- Usability enhancements

Self Service BI would not be possible without a functional data model. Historically, BI projects focused on building data models could take months and even years to develop when working within the rigid structure and constraints of a corporate business intelligence environment. Unfortunately, studies show that about fifty percent of all BI projects fail, and that these projects either do not complete or don't deliver on promised deliverables at the completion of the project.

Fortunately, Power BI Desktop provides you with a much more agile approach to building your data model, and instead of months or years, you can now build your data model in hours or days.

Building relationships

One could argue that the building of relationships is the most important piece of Power BI Desktop. It is this process, the building of relationships, that makes everything else work like magic in Power BI. The automatic filtering of visuals and reports, the ease in which you can author DAX measures, and the ability to quickly connect disparate data sources are all made possible through properly built relationships in the data model.

Sometimes, Power BI Desktop will create the relationships for you automatically. It is important to verify these *auto-detected relationships* to ensure accuracy.

There are a few characteristics of relationships that you should be aware of, and that will be discussed in this section:

- Auto-detected relationships
- There may be only one active relationship between two tables
- There may be an unlimited number of in-active relationships between two tables
- Relationships may only be built on a single column, not multiple columns
- Relationships automatically filter from the one side of the relationship to the many side
- Relationships cannot be built directly between tables that have a many-to-many relationship

Open up the .pbix file Chapter 3 - Building the Data Model.pbix found in your class files.

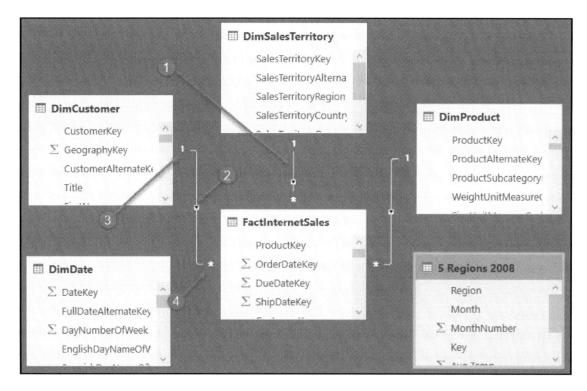

Figure 1-pbix file____

Let's take a closer look at each of the four items highlighted in the preceding screenshot:

1. **Relationship**: The line between two tables represents that a relationship exists
2. **Direction**: The arrow indicates which direction that filtering will occur
3. **One side**: The 1 indicates the Customer table as the one side of the relationship
4. **Many side**: The * indicates that the FactInternetSales table is the many side of the relationship

The first thing you should do after importing data is to verify that all auto-detected relationships have been created correctly. From the modeling ribbon, select **Manage Relationships**:

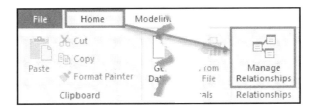

Figure 2-Manage Relationships

This will open up the **Manage Relationships** editor. The relationship editor is where you will go to create new relationships and edit or delete existing relationships. In this demo, the relationship editor will be used to verify the relationships that were automatically created by Power BI Desktop.

Let's take a look at the **Manage Relationships** editor, in which you can manage or perform the following:

- Current relationships in the data model
- Create a new relationship
- Edit existing relationships

- Delete a relationship

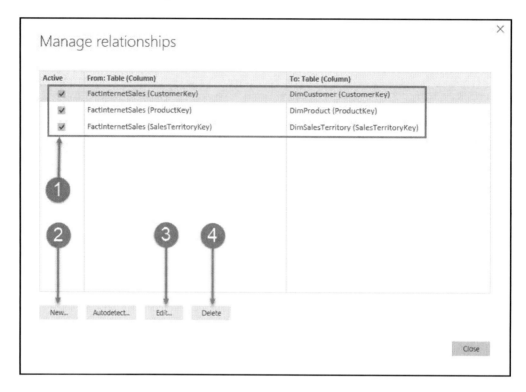

Figure 3- Deleting a Relationship

First, you need to verify auto-detected relationships. The top half of the relationship editor gives you a quick and easy way to see what tables have relationships between them, what columns the relationships have been created on, and if the relationship is an active relationship. We will discuss active and inactive relationships later in this chapter:

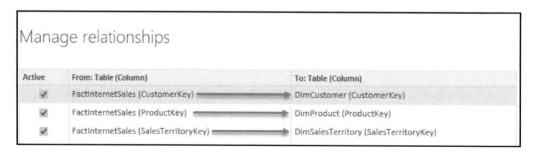

Figure 4-Active Relationshops

Take a look at *Figure 4*, You will see that there are currently three relationships, and all three relationships are currently active. The first relationship is the relationship between the CustomerKey column in the FactInternetSales table and the CustomerKey column in the DimCustomer table. This relationship was created automatically by Power BI Desktop when the tables were imported into the data model, and this is a valid relationship. In fact, all three relationships are valid.

Editing relationships

Now, let's take a look at how to edit an existing relationship. In this example, you will edit the relationship between **FactInternetSales** and **DimCustomer**. To edit an existing relationship, select that relationship and then click on **Edit...**. See *Figure 5*, here:

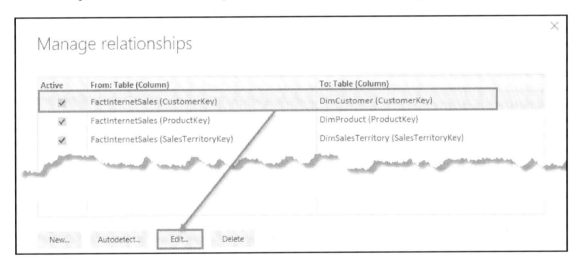

Figure 5-Editing a relationship

Once you select **Edit...** you will receive a new dialog box; this is the **Edit Relationship** editor. In this view, you will see how to change an existing relationship, how to change a relationship to active or inactive, and the cardinality of the current relationship; this is also where you can change the cross filter direction:

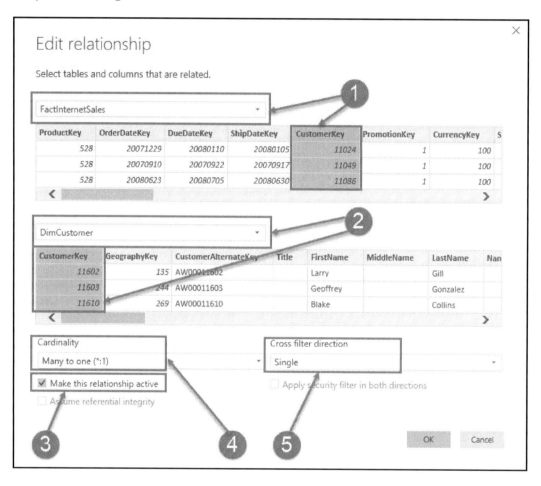

Figure 6-Editing a relationship

There are five things we want to look at in the edit relationship window:

1. This identifies the **FactInternetSales** table and the column that the relationship was built on.
2. This identifies the DimCustomer table and the column that the relationship was built on.

2. This checkbox identifies whether the relationship is active or inactive.

3. This is the current cardinality between the two tables. Here we see that there is a many-to-one relationship between `FactInternetSales` and `DimCustomer`. Power BI does an excellent job of identifying the correct cardinality, but it is important to always verify that the cardinality is correct.

4. The cross filter direction can be single or both. The one side of a relationship always filters the many side of the relationship, and this is the default behavior in Power BI. The cross filter option allows you to change this behavior. Cross filtering will be discussed later in this chapter.

If you need to change the relationship of an existing relationship, then you would do that in the edit relationship editor seen in *Figure 6*. To change the column that a relationship has been created on, simply select a different column. It is important to point out that a relationship between two tables may only be created on a single column. Therefore, if you have a multiple column key, also known as a composite key, then you would need to first combine those keys into a single column before creating your relationship. You saw how to combine columns in the previous chapter.

Creating a new relationship

In the previous section, you saw how to verify existing relationships, and even how to edit them. In this section, you are going to learn how to create a new relationship. There are six tables in the data model so far, and Power BI created a relationship for all the tables, except for two. Let's start by creating a relationship to the `DimDate` table.

The `FactInternetSales` table stores three different dates: `OrderDate`, `ShipDate`, and `DueDate`. There can be only one active relationship between two tables in Power BI, and all filtering occurs through the active relationship. In other words, which date do you want to see your total sales, profit, and profit margin calculations on? If it's `OrderDate`, then your relationship will be on the `OrderDate` column from the `FactInternetSales` table to the `FullDateAlternateKey` column in the `DimDate` table. To create a new relationship, open "manage relationships" from the home ribbon.

Now, let's create a relationship from the `OrderDate` column in `FactInternetSales` to the `FullDateAlternateKey` column in `DimDate`. With the manage relationship editor open, click on **New...** to create a new relationship:

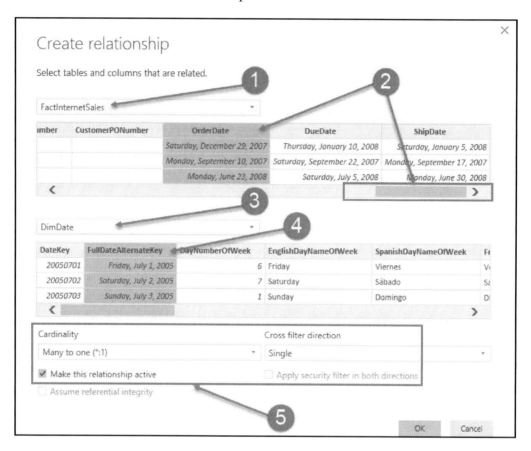

Figure 7- Creating a new relationship

Complete the following steps to create a new relationship:

1. Select `FactInternetSales` from the list of tables in the dropdown
2. Select `OrderDate` from the list of columns, and use the scroll bar to scroll all the way to the right
3. Select `DimDate` from the next in the drop-down list
4. Select `FullDateAlternateKey` from the list of columns

5. The cardinality, cross filter direction, and whether the relationship is active or inactive is updated automatically by Power BI; remember to always verify these items.
6. Click **OK** to close the editor

Congratulations, you have created your first relationship with Power BI!

Working with complex relationships

There are many complex scenarios that need to be addressed when building a data model, and Power BI is no different in this regard. In this section, you will learn how to handle many-to-many relationships and role-playing tables in Power BI.

Many-to-many relationships

Once relationships have been defined in your data model, filtering occurs automatically and this adds a tremendous amount of value to Power BI. However, the analytical value achieved through many-to-many relationships does not happen automatically.

Before you can learn how to handle many-to-many relationships in Power BI, you must first understand the basic behavior of filtering. Let's take a minor detour to explain how filtering works. Filtering will be discussed in more detail in the next chapter. In *Figure 8*, the total **SalesAmount** of all transactions is $29,358,677.22. The table visual you see in *Figure 8* is simply the sum of the column **SalesAmount** from the **FactInternetSales** table:

Figure 8- SalesAmount

To view the total **SalesAmount** for all transactions broken down by country, all you would need to do is simply add the **SalesTerritoryCountry** column from the **DimSalesTerritory** table. This behavior in Power BI is awesome, and this is automatic filtering at work. Take a look at *Figure 9*:

Figure 9-Viewing total sales amount

Please note that this only works because a valid relationship exists between the **FactInternetSales** and **DimSalesTerritory** tables. If a relationship had not been created, or if the relationship created was invalid, then you would get entirely different results and they would be confusing. Let's take a look at what would happen if no relationship had previously existed. In *Figure 10*, the country has been removed and replaced with the Temperature Range column from the **5 Regions 2008** table:

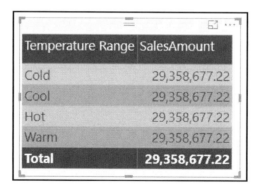

Figure 10-Replacing Country with Temperature range

Notice how the total sales amount is repeated for each temperature range. This behavior indicates that the **5 Regions 2008** table is unable to filter the **FactInternetSales** table. This inability to filter can happen for a number of different reasons, and here are a few:

- Because a relationship does not exist between the tables
- Because an existing relationship is invalid
- Because an existing relationship does not allow the filtering to pass through an intermediate table

If you see the repeated value behavior demonstrated in Figure 10, then go back to the relationship view and verify that all relationships have been created and are valid.

Cross-filtering direction

Now that you understand the basics of automatic filtering in Power BI, let's take a look at an example of a many-to-many relationship. **DimProduct** and **DimCustomer** have a many-to-many relationship. A product can be sold to many customers. For example, bread can be sold to Jessica, Kim, and Tyrone. A customer can purchase many products. Kim could purchase bread, milk, and cheese.

A bridge table can be used to store the relationship between two tables that have a many-to-many relationship, just like tools you have worked with in the past.

The relationship between **DimProduct** and **DimCustomer** is stored in the **FactInternetSales** table. The **FactInternetSales** table is a large many-to-many bridge table:

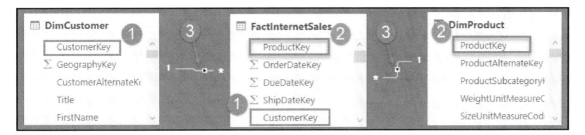

Figure 11-Relationship between DimCustomer and FactInternetSales

Figure 11 shows the relationship between these two tables; see the following explanation for the numbered points:

1. The relationship between **DimCustomer** and **FactInternetSales**
2. The relationship between **DimProduct** and **FactInternetSales**
3. The cross filter direction is set to single

The following report displays the total sales, total transactions, and customer count for each product:

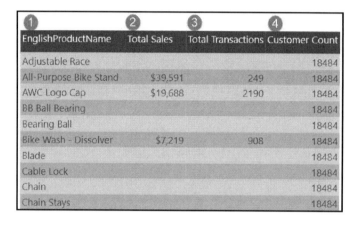

Figure 12- Customer Count for each product

Let's take a closer look at Figure 12, and note the numbered points:

1. **Product Name** from the **DimProduct** table
2. **Total Sales** is the SUM of the **Sales Amount** column from the **FactInternetSales** table
3. **Total Transactions** is the number of corresponding transactions from the **FactInternetSales** table
4. Customer Count is the COUNT of the **CustomerKey** column from the **DimCustomer** table

Total Sales and Total Transactions are returning the correct results for each product. Customer Count is returning the same value for all products (18,484). This is due to the way that filtering works. The calculations for **Total Sales** and **Total Transactions** are derived from columns or rows that come from the **FactInternetSales** table. The Product table has a one-to-many relationship with Internet Sales, and therefore filtering occurs automatically. This explains why those two calculations are being filtered properly, but it does not explain why the count of customers is returning the same repeated value for all products, not entirely anyway.

Let's take another look at the relationship between **DimProduct** and **DimCustomer**. You will notice in the following image that the relationship between these two tables flows through the **FactInternetSales** table. This is because they have a many-to-many relationship. In this scenario, the table **FactInternetSales** is acting as a large many-to-many bridge table. DimProduct filters FactInternet Sales. DimCustomer also filters FactInternetSales, and FactInternetSales is currently unable to filter the customer table:

Figure 13

The repeated value for customer count occurs because **FactInternetSales** is unable to filter the **DimCustomer** table. **DimProduct** filters **FactInternetSales**, and a list of transactions are returned for each product. Unfortunately, the filtering does not pass from **FactInternetSales** to **DimCustomer**. This is because **FactInternetSales** is on the many side of the relationship with **DimCustomer**. Therefore, when our calculation performs a count on the customer key, the table is not filtered and the calculation sees every customer key in the **DimCustomer** table (18,484).

Do you remember the cross-filter direction property that was briefly covered earlier in this chapter? That little property is there to provide many-to-many support. By simply enabling cross-filtering in both directions, the **FactInternetSales** table will be able to filter the customer table and the customer count will work.

Enabling filtering from the many side of a relationship

To enable cross-filtering, click on Manage Relationships from the home ribbon; this will launch the manage relationship editor. Find the relationship between **FactInternetSales** and **DimCustomer**, and then click **Edit**.

Once the relationship editor has launched, change the cross-filter direction from single to both:

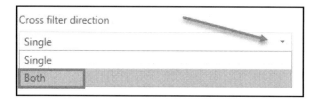

Figure 14- Changing the Cross filter direction

Back in the report view, you will now see the correct customer count for each product:

EnglishProductName	Total Sales	Total Transactions	Customer Count
All-Purpose Bike Stand	$39,591	249	243
AWC Logo Cap	$19,688	2190	2132
Bike Wash - Dissolver	$7,219	908	875
Classic Vest, L	$12,383	195	195
Classic Vest, M	$12,637	199	199
Classic Vest, S	$10,668	168	168
Fender Set - Mountain	$46,620	2121	2110
Half-Finger Gloves, L	$10,849	443	437

Figure 15-Customer Count for each product

Do not enable cross-filtering for your date table. In order for some DAX calculations to work properly, the date table must have a contiguous range of dates.

Role-playing tables

A role-playing table is a table that can play multiple roles, and this helps to reduce data redundancy. Most often, the Date table is a role-playing table. For example, the **FactInternetSales** table has three dates to track the processing of an order. There is the Order Date, Ship Date, and Due Date and, without role-playing tables, you would need to have three separate date tables instead of just one. The additional tables take up valuable resources, such as memory, as well as add an extra layer of administrative upkeep.

Each of these dates is very important to different people and different departments within an organization. For example, the finance department may wish to see total sales and profit by the date that a product was purchased, the order date. However, your shipping department may wish to see product quantity based on the ship date. How do you accommodate requests from different departments in a single data model?

One of the things I loved about working with SQL Server Analysis Services Multidimensional was the ease with which it handled role-playing tables; perhaps you also come from a background where you have worked with tools that had built-in support for Role-Playing tables. Unfortunately, Role-Playing tables are not natively supported in Power BI; this is because all filtering in Power BI occurs through the active relationship and you can only have one active relationship between two tables.

There are generally two ways you can handle role-playing tables in Power BI:

1. Importing the table multiple times and creating individual active relationships.
2. Using DAX and inactive relationships to create calculations that show calculations by different dates.

The first way, and the method we will show here, is importing the table multiple times. Yes, this means that it will take up more resources. The data model will have three date tables, one table to support each date in the FactInternetSales table. Each date table will have a single active relationship to the FactInternetSales table.

Some of the benefits of importing the table multiple times are as follows:

- It is easier to train and acclimate end users with the data model. For example, if you want to see sales and profit by the ship date, then you would simply use the date attributes from the ship date table in your reports.
- Most, if not all, DAX measures will work across all date tables, so no need for creating new measures.
- The analytical value of putting different dates in a matrix. For example, sales ordered and sales shipped by date.

Some of the cons of importing the table multiples times are:

- Resources. Additional memory and space will be used.
- Administrative changes. Any modifications made to one table will need to be repeated for all tables, as these tables are not linked. For example, if you create a hierarchy in one table, then you would need to create a hierarchy in all date tables.

The report in Figure 16 shows total sales and total transactions by year, but which year? Is this the year that a product was purchased or the year a product was shipped? The active relationship is on order date, so the report is displaying the results based on when the product was purchased:

CalendarYear	Total Sales	Total Transactions
2005	$3,266,374	1013
2006	$6,530,344	2677
2007	$9,791,060	24443
2008	$9,770,900	32265
Total	**$29,358,677**	**60398**

Figure 16-Total sales and total transactions by year

Importing the date table

In this section, we are going to import a date table to support analyzing data based on when an order shipped. From the get data option, select excel and open the AdventureWorksDW excel file; the file can be found in the directory location, C:\Packt\Power BI Quick Start\Data\

Next, select **DimDate** from the list of tables, and then click load:

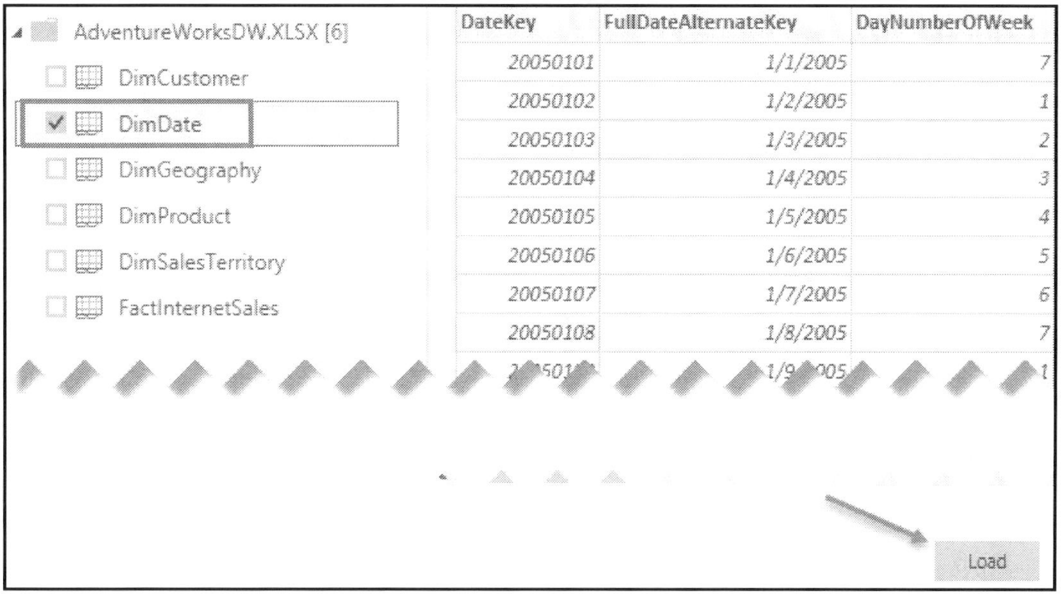

DateKey	FullDateAlternateKey	DayNumberOfWeek
20050101	1/1/2005	7
20050102	1/2/2005	1
20050103	1/3/2005	2
20050104	1/4/2005	3
20050105	1/5/2005	4
20050106	1/6/2005	5
20050107	1/7/2005	6
20050108	1/8/2005	7

AdventureWorksDW.XLSX [6]
- DimCustomer
- ✓ DimDate
- DimGeography
- DimProduct
- DimSalesTerritory
- FactInternetSales

Load

Figure 17- Select DimDate from the list of tables

Now that the data has been imported, the next step is creating a valid relationship. Select Manage Relationships, found on the home ribbon, to launch the relationship editor. Click new to create a new relationship. Complete the following steps:

1. Select **FactInternetSales** from the drop-down list.
2. Select the **ShipDate** column; use the scroll bar to scroll all the way to right.
3. Select **DimDate** (2) from the drop-down list.
4. Select the **FullDateAlternateKey** column.
5. Click **OK** to close the create relationship window.

I took the liberty of changing the table and column names here, for clarity. You will learn how to rename tables and columns in the following *Usability enhancements* section.

1. **DimDate** has been renamed **Order Date.**
2. **DimDate** (2) has been renamed Ship Date.

The data model now has two date tables, each with an active relationship to the **FactInternetSales** table. If you wish to see sales by order year then you would bring in the year column from the **Order Date** table, and if you wish to see sales by the ship year, then you would bring in the year column from the Ship Date table:

Figure 18-Displaying ship year column

Importing the same table multiple times is generally the preferred method when two tables have multiple relationships between them. This method is easy to explain to end users and allows you to reuse most, if not all, of your existing DAX calculations.

The alternative method is to create inactive relationships and then create new calculations (measures) using the Data Analysis Expression (DAX) language. This method of leveraging inactive relationships can become overwhelming from an administrative point of view. Imagine having to create copies of the existing measures in the data model for each relationship between two tables. In the current data model, **FactInternetSales** stores three dates, and this would possibly mean having to create and maintain three copies of each measure, one to support each date.

Usability enhancements

Usability enhancements are those enhancements that can significantly improve the overall user experience when interacting with the data model. In order to ensure a successful handoff and adoption of the work you have done, it is important to not overlook these rather basic improvements.

In this section, we are going to cover the following usability enhancements:

1. Hiding tables and columns
2. Renaming tables and columns
3. Changing the default summarization property
4. How to display one column but sort by another
5. Setting the data category of fields
6. How to create hierarchies

Hiding tables and columns

Some tables are available in the data model simply in a support capacity, and would never be used in a report. For example, you may have a table to support many-to-many relationships, weighted allocation, or even dynamic security. Likewise, some columns are necessary for creating relationships in the data model but would not add any value when added to a report. Tables or columns that will not be used for reporting purposes should be hidden from the report view to reduce complexity and improve the user experience.

To hide a column or table, simply right-click on the object you wish to hide, and then select **Hide in report view**. If you are in the report view already, the available option will simply say **Hide**.

Navigate to the relationship view, find the **FactInternetSales** table, and right-click on **ProductKey,** then select **Hide in report view**:

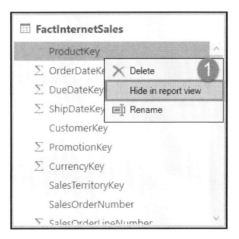

Figure 19-Select Hide in report view

Columns that are hidden are still visible in the data and relationship views, but they have slightly lighter text than columns that are not hidden, as you can see in Figure 20:

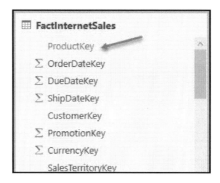

Figure 20-Hidden Columns

Next, go to each table and hide all remaining key columns, except for **FullDateAlternateKey**.

Renaming tables and columns

The renaming of tables and columns is an important step in making your data model easy to use. Different departments often have different terms for the same entity, therefore it is important to consider multiple departments when renaming objects. For example, you may have a column with a list of customer names and you decide to name this column Customer. However, the sales team may have named that column Prospect or Client, or any number of other terms. Remember to keep your end users and consumers of your reports in mind when renaming tables and columns.

You may rename tables or columns in the report, data, or relationship view. Navigate to the relationship view and right-click on FactInternetSales, then select Rename:

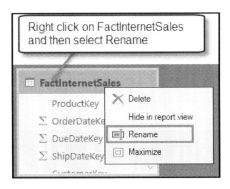

Figure 21-Renaming FactInternetSales

Rename this table to Internet Sales. Now, rename the other tables, removing the Dim prefix and adding spaces where applicable. You can use the table here for reference:

FactInternetSales	Internet Sales
DimDate	Date (Order)
DimDate (2)	Date (Ship
DimProduct	Product
DimCustomer	Customer
DimSalesTerritory	Sales Territory
5 Regions 2008	Temperature

The next step is necessary, but could be a somewhat tedious process. If you come from a programming or development background, then you are used to eliminating spaces in table and column names. End users and consumers of reports will expect to see spaces and, for that reason, it is recommended to add spaces where applicable. Spaces need to be added to any column that is visible, not hidden, in the report view. To rename a column, right-click on it and then select **Rename**. In the following screenshot, spaces have been added to **SalesOrderNumber** and **SalesOrderLineNumber**.

Complete the following steps to rename the rest of your columns:

1. Repeat this process of adding spaces for the remaining columns in each table
2. Rename **FullDateAlternateKey** to simply `Date`:

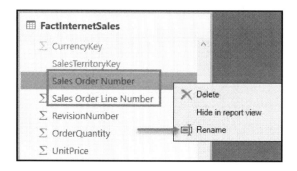

Figure 22-Renaming columns in each table

Default summarization

By default, Power BI assigns a default summarization to numeric columns, and this default summarization is usually a sum operation. Columns that have been assigned a default summarization are denoted by Power BI with a Sigma symbol (Σ). **DateKey**, **Day Number of Week**, **Day Number of Month**, **Day Number of Year**, and **Week Number of Year** have all been assigned a default summarization by Power BI in the following screenshot:

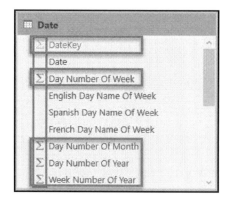

Figure 23-Default assigned columns for sumarization

This automatic assignment of default summarizations can cause a lot of confusion to report developers in Power BI. Columns that have a default summarization assigned will be automatically aggregated with their assigned default summarization when added to a report. The columns identified in Figure 23 are generally descriptive attributes that help to explain the data; these columns would rarely be aggregated. Take a look at the following screenshot:

Figure 24-Year column from date table

In *Figure 24*, the **Year** column from the date table has been added into a table visual, and the expected behavior is to see a distinct list of years (2005, 2006, 2007, 2008, 2009, and 2010). Instead, a value of 4,398,433 is returned. Instead of returning a distinct list, the report returns a sum of all records from the year column in the date table. See the screenshot and steps shown next to adjust the default summarization:

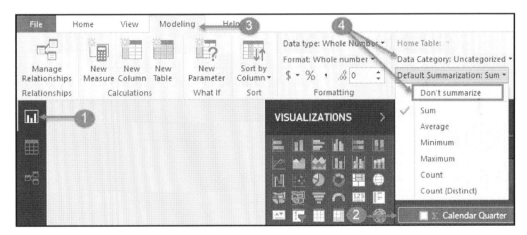

Figure 25-Adjust the default summarization

The preceding screenshot walks through changing the default summarization, with detailed steps listed here:

1. Select the report view from the left navigation bar.
2. Expand the date table and select Calendar Quarter, highlighted by a yellow box.
3. Select the modeling ribbon.
4. Click the dropdown for Default Summarization, and select Don't summarize.

Repeat the above process for each column in the date table that has been assigned a default summarization by Power BI.

How to display one column but sort by another

Oftentimes, you want to display the name of one column but sort by another. For example, the month name is sorted alphabetically when added to a report visual; see the following screenshot as an example:

Figure 26-Month names sorted alphabetically when added to a report visual

The desired behavior is for the month to be sorted chronologically instead. Therefore, the report should display the month name but sort by the month number of year. Let's take a look at how to change the sorting:

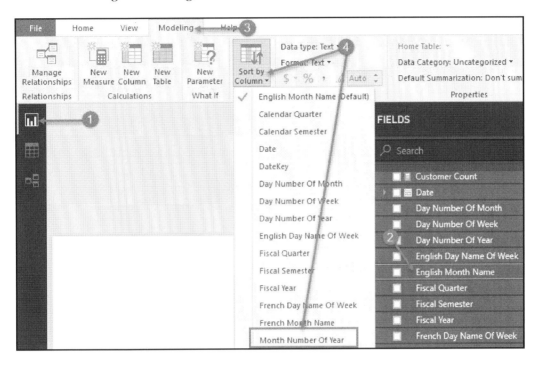

Figure 27-Changing the sort order of a column

In order to change the sort order of a column, complete the following steps:

1. Select the report view from the left navigation bar.
2. Expand the date table and select **English Month Name**, highlighted by a yellow box.
3. Select the modeling ribbon.
4. Click the dropdown for **Sort by Column**, and select **Month Number of Year**.

Data categorization

Power BI makes some assumptions about your columns based on data types, column names, and relationships in the data model. These assumptions are used in the report view when building visualizations to improve your default experience with the tool. Once you start building visualizations, you will notice that Power BI selects different types of visuals for different columns; this is by design. Power BI also decides column placement within the fields section of a visual, and you will learn more about the creation of visuals in Chapter 5, *Visualizing Data*. As you saw previously in this chapter, when Power BI detects a column that has numeric values, a default aggregation is assigned. Power BI assumes you will want to aggregate that data, and will automatically place these numeric columns into the Values area of a report visual.

The classification of data allows you to improve the user experience as well as improve accuracy. There are quite a few different options available for data categorization, thirteen in fact. Take a look at the options available in the following screenshot:

Figure 28-Options for data categorization

The most common use for data categorization is the classification of geographical data. When geographical data is added to a map, Bing maps may have to make some assumptions about how to map that data. This can sometimes cause inaccurate results. However, through data classification, you can reduce and possibly eliminate inaccurate results.

One method I have found extremely useful is combining multiple address columns (City, State) into a single column, and assigning the new column a data categorization of "Place". I have used this method with great success. See the following blog post for more tips on mapping geographical data:
`https://tinyurl.com/pbiqs-categoryplace`.

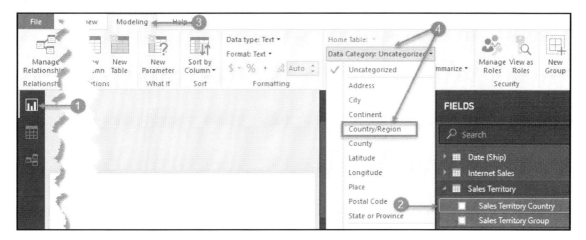

Figure 29-Modifying the date category

Follow the steps here to modify the data category:

1. Select the report view from the left navigation bar.
2. Expand the **Sales Territory** table and select **Sales Territory Country**, highlighted by a yellow box.
3. Select the modeling ribbon.
4. Click the dropdown for **Data Category**, and select **Country/Region**.

Creating hierarchies

Predefining hierarchies can provide several key benefits. Some of those benefits are listed here:

1. Hierarchies organize attributes and show relationships in the data
2. Hierarchies allow for easy drag and drop interactivity
3. Hierarchies add significant analytical value to the visualization layer through drilling down and rolling up data, as necessary

Hierarchies store information about relationships in the data, that users may not have otherwise known. I remember when I was working for a client in the telecommunication industry and they had Base Transceiver Stations (BTS) and Sectors, and without looking at my notes, I could never remember the correct order. Did a BTS contain multiple sectors, or did a sector contain multiple base transceiver stations? Once the hierarchy was added to the data model, I no longer had to worry about remembering the relationship because the relationship was stored in the hierarchy. Here is a list of common hierarchies:

1. **Category | Subcategory | Product**
2. **Country | State | City**
3. **Year | Quarter | Month | Day**

Hierarchies may only be created in either the report or data view. In order to create a new hierarchy, complete the following steps:

1. Expand the **Sales Territory** table.
2. Right-click on the **Sales Territory Country** column.
3. Select **New Hierarchy**:

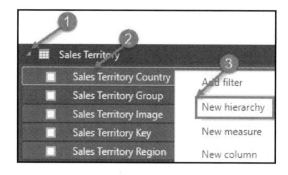

Figure 30-Create a new hierarchy

A new hierarchy has been created with a single column, and given a default name of **Sales Territory Country Hierarchy**:

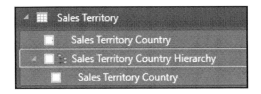

Figure 31-New hierarchy created

First, right-click on the Sales Territory Country Hierarchy and rename it to **Sales Territory Drilldown**. The next step is to add additional columns/attributes to the hierarchy. Complete the following steps:

1. Right click on **Sales Territory Region**.
2. Click on **Add to Hierarchy**.
3. Select **Sales Territory Drilldown**.
4. Repeat steps 1-3 for Sales Territory Group:

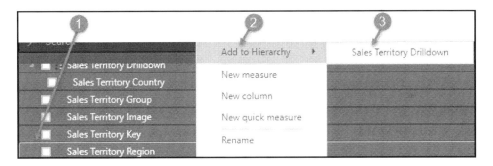

Figure 32-Adding columns/attributes to the hierarchy

The completed hierarchy can be seen in the following screenshot. However, the order of the attributes is incorrect; the order should be **Sales Territory Group** | **Sales Territory Country** | **Sales Territory Region**:

Figure 33-Completed hierarchy

To correct the order of the attributes:

1. Right-click on **Sales Territory Group**.
2. Click **Move Up**.
3. Repeat steps 1 and 2:

Figure 34-Correct the order of attributes

Summary

In this chapter, you learned how to build relationships between the different tables within your data model. These relationships, combined with simple, yet critical, usability enhancements, allow you to build a data model that is both coherent and intelligent. Historically, business intelligence projects cost significant resources in terms of time and money. Through a self-service approach to BI, you now have the tools necessary to build your own BI project within hours or even minutes.

4
Leveraging DAX

Data analysis expressions (DAX) is a formula language that made its debut back in 2010 with the release of Power Pivot within Excel. Much of DAX is similar to Excel's functions, and therefore learning DAX is an easy transition for Excel users and power users. In fact, DAX is so similar to Excel that I have seen new students become comfortable with the language and begin writing DAX within minutes.

The goal of this chapter is to introduce you to DAX and give you the confidence to start exploring this language on your own. Because of the brevity of this chapter, there will not be any discussions on in-depth DAX concepts and theory. There are, of course, many other books that are dedicated to just that.

Now, let's take a look at what is covered in this chapter:

- Building calculated columns
- Calculated measures – the basics
- Calculated measures – filter context
- Calculated measures – time intelligence

Building calculated columns

Open the pbix file Chapter 4 – Leveraging DAX from the book files

Calculated columns are stored in the table in which they are assigned, and the values are static until the data is refreshed. You will learn more about refreshing data in a later chapter.

There are many use cases for calculated columns, but the two most common are as follows:

- Descriptive attributes
- Concatenated key columns

Now you are going to create your first calculated column. Before you get started, though, you need to first know that Power BI Desktop has IntelliSense. IntelliSense will help you out a lot when writing code, as you will discover very soon. This built-in functionality will autocomplete your code as you go, and will also help you explore and discover new functions in the DAX language. In order to take advantage of IntelliSense, you simply need to start typing in the formula bar. Now you are ready to start writing DAX!

Click on the **Data View**—this is located on the left side of the Power BI Desktop screen. Next, click on the customer table from the **Fields** list. Once the customer table has been selected, click **New Column**—this is found under the modeling ribbon, as shown in the following screenshot:

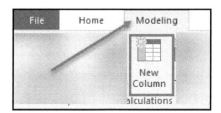

Figure 1- New column

You will now see the text **Column** = in the formula bar. First, name the new column by replacing the default text of **Column** with **Full Name**. Then, move your cursor to after the equals sign and type a single quote character. Immediately after typing the single quote character, a list of autocomplete options will appear preceding the formula bar. This is IntelliSense at work. The first option in this list is the name of the table you currently have selected—**Customer**. Click the *Tab* key and the name of the table will automatically be added to the formula bar, as shown in the following screenshot:

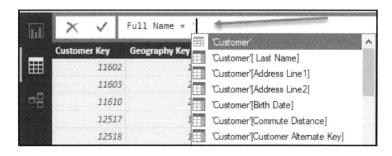

Figure 2-Adding name of the table

At some point, you will inevitably discover that you can reference just the column name. As a best practice, we recommend always referencing both the table and column name anytime you use a column in your DAX code.

Next, type an opening square bracket into the formula bar followed by a capital letter F, making **[F**. Once again, you will immediately be presented with autocomplete options. The list of options has been limited to only columns that contain the letter f, and the first option available from the drop down is **First Name**. Click *tab* to autocomplete. The formula bar should now contain the following formula:

Full Name = 'Customer'[First Name]

The next step is to add a space, followed by the last name. There are two options in DAX for combining string values. The first option is the `concatenate` function. Unfortunately, `concatenate` only accepts two parameters; therefore, if you have more than two parameters, your code will require multiple `concatenate` function calls. On the other hand, you also have the option of using the ampersand sign (`&`) to combine strings. The ampersand will first take both input parameters and convert them into strings. After this data conversion step, the two strings are then combined into one. Let's continue with the rest of the expression. Remember to use the built-in autocomplete functionality to help you write code.

Next, add a space and the last name column. To add a space—or any string literal value for that matter—into a DAX formula, you will use quotes on both sides of the string. For example, " " inserts a space between the first and last name columns. The completed DAX formula will look like the following:

```
Full Name = 'Customer'[First Name] & " " & 'Customer'[Last Name]
```

String functions – Month, Year

Now that you have completed your first calculated column, let's build a calculated column that stores the month–year value. The goal is to return a month–year column with the two-digit month and four-digit year separated by a dash, making "MM-YYYY". Let's build this calculation incrementally.

Select the **Date** (order) table and then click **New Column** from the modeling ribbon. Write the following code in the formula bar and then hit *Enter*:

```
Month Year = 'Date (Order)'[Month Number of Year]
```

As you begin validating the code, you will notice that this only returns the single-digit month with no leading zero. Your next attempt may look something like the following:

```
Month Year = "0" & 'Date (Order)'[Month Number of Year]
```

This will work for single-digit months; however, double-digit months will now return three digits. Take a look at the following screenshot:

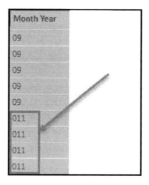

Figure 3-Displaying Month Year

To improve upon this and only return the two-digit month, you can use the `RIGHT`function. The RIGHT function returns a specified number of characters from the right side of a string. Modify your existing DAX formula to look like the following:

```
Month Year = RIGHT("0" & 'Date (Order)'[Month Number of Year], 2)
```

For a full list of text functions in DAX, please go to the following link: https://tinyurl.com/pbiqs-text

The rest of this formula can be completed quite easily. First, to add a dash, the following DAX code can be used:

```
Month Year = RIGHT("0" & 'Date (Order)'[Month Number of Year], 2) & "-"
```

Complete the Month Year formula by combining the current string with the calendar year column:

```
RIGHT("0" & 'Date (Order)'[Month Number of Year], 2) & "-" & 'Date
(Order)'[Year])
```

You may have noticed that the Year column has a data type of a whole number, and you may have expected that this numeric value would need to be converted to a string prior to the `combine` operation. However, remember that the ampersand operator will automatically convert both inputs into a string before performing the combine operation!

Format function – Month Year

As with any other language, you will find that there are usually multiple ways to do something. Now you are going to learn how to perform the calculation that we saw in the previous section using the FORMAT function. The FORMAT function allows you to take a number or date column and customize it in a number of ways. A side effect of the FORMAT function is that the resulting data type will be text. Let's perform the preceding calculation again, but this time using the FORMAT function.

Make sure you have the **Date** (order) table selected, and then click on **Create a New Calculated Column** by selecting **New Column** from the modeling ribbon. In the formula bar, write the following expression:

```
Month Year Format = FORMAT('Date (Order)'[Date], "MM-YYYY")
```

If you would like to take a full look at all the custom formatting options available using the FORMAT function, please take a look at `https://tinyurl.com/pbiqs-format`.

Age calculation

Next, you are going to determine the age of each customer. The **Customer** table currently contains a column with the birth date for each customer. This column, along with the TODAY function and some DAX, will allow you to determine each customer's age. Your first attempt at this calculation may be to use the `DATEDIFF` function in a calculation that looks something like the following:

Customer Age = DATEDIFF('Customer'[Birth Date], TODAY(), YEAR)

The `TODAY` function returns the current date and time. The `DATEDIFF` function returns the count of the specified interval between two dates; however, it does not look at the day and month, and therefore does not always return the correct age for each customer.

Let's rewrite the previous DAX formula in a different way. In this example, you are going to learn how to use conditional logic and the FORMAT function to return the proper customer age. Please keep in mind, that there are many ways to perform this calculation.

Select the **Customer Age** column from the previous step and rewrite the formula to look like the following:

```
Customer Age =
IF(
    FORMAT('Customer'[Birth Date], "MMDD") <= FORMAT(TODAY(), "MMDD"), //Logical Test
    DATEDIFF('Customer'[Birth Date], TODAY(), YEAR),                   //Result If True
    DATEDIFF('Customer'[Birth Date], TODAY(), YEAR) -1)               //Result If False
```

Figure 4-Select Customer age and rewrite the formula

Formatting code is very important for readability and maintaining code. Power BI Desktop has a built-in functionality to help out with code formatting. When you type *Shift + Enter* to navigate down to the next line in your formula bar, your code will be indented automatically where applicable.

When completed, the preceding code returns the correct age for each customer. The FORMAT function is used to return the two-digit month and two-digit day for each date (the birth date and today's date). Following the logical test portion of the IF statement are two expressions. The first expression is triggered if the logical test evaluates to true, and the second expression is triggered if the result of the test is false. Therefore, if the customer's month and day combo is less than or equal to today's month and day, then their birthday has already occurred this year, and the logical test will evaluate to true, which will trigger the first expression. If the customer's birthday has not yet occurred this year, then the second expression will execute.

In the preceding DAX formula, I added comments by using two forward slashes in the code. Comments are descriptive, and are not executed with the rest of the DAX formula. Commenting code is always encouraged, and will make your code more readable and easier to maintain.

SWITCH() – age breakdown

Now that you have the customer's age, it's time to put each customer into an age bucket. For this example, there will be four separate age buckets:

- 18-34
- 35-44
- 45-54
- 55 +

The SWITCH function is preferable to the IF function when performing multiple logical tests in a single DAX formula. This is because the SWITCH function is easier to read and makes debugging code much easier.

With the **Customer** table selected, click New Column from the modeling ribbon. Type in the completed DAX formula for the following example:

```
Age Breakdown =
SWITCH(TRUE(),
    'Customer'[Customer Age] >= 55,  "55 +", //If 55 or older then 55 +
    'Customer'[Customer Age] >= 45, "45-54", //If 45-54 then 45-54
    'Customer'[Customer Age] >= 35, "35-44", //If 35-44 then 35-44
    "18-34")                                 //ELSE, 18-34
```

Figure 5-Completed DAX formula

The preceding formula is very readable and understandable. There are three logical tests, and if a customer age does not evaluate to true on any of those logical tests, then that customer is automatically put into the 18-34 age bucket.

The astute reader may have noticed that the second and third logical tests do not have an upper range assigned. For example, the second test simply checks whether the customer's age is 45 or greater. Naturally, you may assume that a customer whose age is 75 would be incorrectly assigned to the 45–54 age bucket. However, once a row evaluates to true, it is no longer available for subsequent logical tests. Someone who is 75 would have evaluated to true on the first logical test (55 +) and would no longer be available for any further tests.

If you would like a better understanding of using the SWITCH statement instead of nesting multiple IF statements, then you can check out a blog post by Rob Collie at https://tinyurl.com/pbiqs-switch.

Navigation functions – RELATED

It's finally time to create a relationship between the temperature table and internet sales table. The key on the **Temperature** table is a combination of the region name and the month number of the year. This column combination makes a single row unique in this table, as shown in the following screenshot:

Region	Month	MonthNumber	Key	Avg Temp	Temperature Range
Northeast	Jan	1	Northeast1	26.3	Cold
Northeast	Feb	2	Northeast2	25.4	Cold
Northeast	Mar	3	Northeast3	31.4	Cold
Northeast	Apr	4	Northeast4	48.1	Cool

Figure 6-Column combination that makes a single row unique

Unfortunately, neither of those two columns currently exist in the **Internet Sales** table. However, the **Internet Sales** table has a relationship to the **Sales Territory** table, and the **Sales Territory** table has the region. Therefore, you can determine the region for each sale by doing a simple `lookup` operation. Well, it should be that simple, but it's not quite that easy. Let's take a look at why.

Calculated columns do not automatically use the existing relationships in the data model. This is a unique characteristic of calculated columns; calculated measures automatically see and interact with all relationships in the data model. Now let's take a look at why this is important.

In the following screenshot, I have created a new column on the **Internet Sales** table and I am trying to return the region name from the **Sales Territory** table. Take a look at the following screenshot:

```
Temperature Key =
'Sales T
```

Figure 7-Sales Territory table

Note that there is no IntelliSense, and that the autocomplete functionality is unavailable as I type in "**Sales Territory**". The reason for this is because the calculated column cannot see the existing relationships in the data model, and therefore does not automatically return the column you want from another table. There is a much more complicated explanation behind all this, but for now, suffice to say that navigation functions (`RELATED` and `RELATEDTABLE`) allow calculated columns to interact with and use existing relationships.

If I rewrite the following DAX formula with the RELATED function, then you will notice that IntelliSense has returned, along with the autocomplete functionality that was previously discussed:

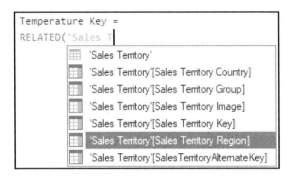

Figure 8-Temperature key column

Now it's time to create a **Temperature Key** column on the **Internet Sales** table. Create a new column on the **Internet Sales** table and then type in the following DAX formula:

```
Temperature Key =
RELATED('Sales Territory'[Sales Territory Region]) & //Return the region from Sales Territory table
RELATED('Date (Order)'[Month Number Of Year])        //Return the Month number of year from the Date table
```

Figure 9-Temperature Key column on the Internet Sales table

Now that the temperature key has been created on the **Internet Sales** table, let's create the relationship. Click **Manage Relationships** from the home ribbon and then click **New...** to open the **Create Relationship** window. Then complete the following steps to create a new relationship. The relevant fields and entries for each step are marked out on the following screenshot:

1. Select **Internet Sales** from the first drop-down selection list
2. Select the **Temperature Key** from the list of columns
3. Select **Temperature** from the second drop-down selection list (scroll right)
4. Select **Key** from the list of columns

5. Click **OK** to save your new relationship:

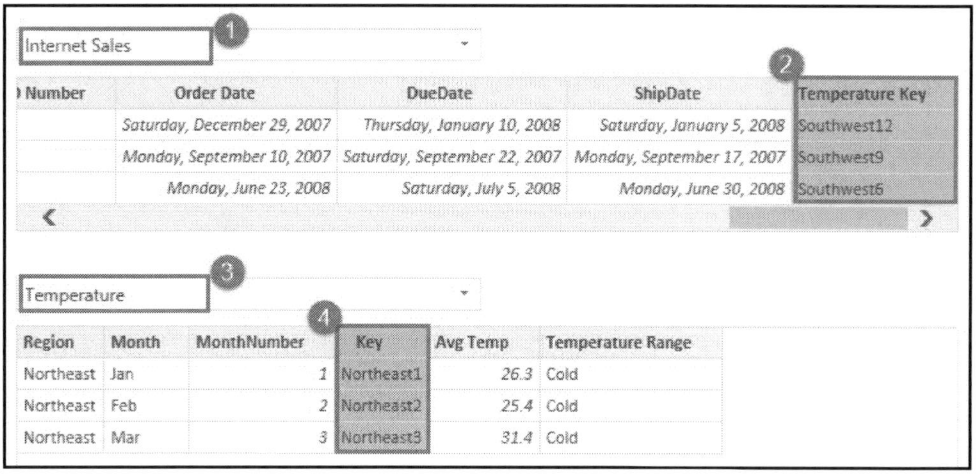

Figure 10-Creating new relationship

Calculated measures – the basics

Calculated measures are very different than calculated columns. Calculated measures are not static, and operate within the current filter context of a report; therefore, calculated measures are dynamic and ever-changing as the filter context changes. You were introduced to filter context in the previous chapter. The concept of the filter context will be slightly expanded on later in this chapter. Calculated measures are powerful analytical tools, and because of the automatic way that measures work with filter contexts they are surprisingly simple to author.

Before you start learning about creating measures, let's first discuss the difference between implicit and explicit measures.

Implicit aggregations occur automatically on columns with numeric data types. You saw this in the previous chapter when the year column was incorrectly aggregated after being added to a report. There are some advantages to this default behavior—for example, if you simply drag the **Sales Amount** column into a report, the value will be automatically aggregated and you won't have to spend time creating a measure. As discussed in the next section, it's generally considered a best practice to create explicit measures in lieu of implicit measures.

An explicit measure allows a user to create a calculated measure, and there are several benefits to using explicit measures:

- Measures can be built on each other
- They encapsulate code, making logic changes less time-consuming
- They centrally define number formatting, creating consistency

Calculated measures can do the following:

- They can be assigned to any table
- They interact with all the relationships in the data model automatically, unlike calculated columns.
- They are not materialized in a column, and therefore cannot be validated in the **Data View**

Calculated measure – basic aggregations

In this section, you are going to create four simple calculated measures:

- Total Sales
- Total Cost
- Profit
- Profit Margin

Total Sales

To create your first measure, select the **Internet Sales** table and then click **New Measure...** from the modeling ribbon. In the formula bar, type the following code and hit *Enter*:

```
Total Sales = SUM('Internet Sales'[Sales Amount])
```

One of the benefits of creating explicit measures is the ability to centralize formatting. Once the measure has been created, navigate to the modeling ribbon and change the formatting to **$ English (United States)**, as shown in the following screenshot:

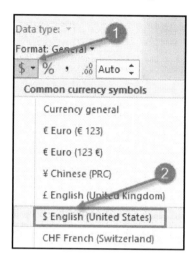

Figure 11-Change formatting to $ English(United States)

Total Cost

Now let's create the Total Cost measure. Once again, this is a simple SUM operation. Click **New Measure...** from the modeling ribbon and type in the following DAX formula:

```
Total Cost = SUM('Internet Sales'[Total Product Cost])
```

Remember to apply formatting to this new measure; it is easy to miss this step when learning to create measures. The formatting should be **$ English (United States)**.

Profit

Profit is the next measure you will create. You may attempt to write something such as the following:

```
Profit = SUM('Internet Sales'[Sales Amount]) - SUM('Internet
Sales'[Total Product Cost])
```

This calculation would be technically correct; however, it's not the most efficient way to write code. In fact, another benefit of building explicit measures is that they can be built on top of each other. Reusing existing calculated measures will make the code more readable, and make code changes easier and less time consuming. Imagine for a moment that you discovered that the Total Sales calculation is not correct. If you encapsulated all this logic in a single measure and reused that measure in your other measures, then you need only change the original measure, and any updates would be pushed to all other measures.

Now it's time to create the Profit measure. select your **Internet Sales** table and then click on **New Measure...** from the modeling ribbon. Type the following into the formula bar—remember to format it:

```
Profit = [Total Sales] - [Total Cost]
```

This calculation returns the same results as the original attempt. The difference is that now you are reusing measures that were already created in the data model. You may have noticed that I referenced the name of the measure without the table name. When referencing explicit measures in your code, it is considered a best practice to exclude the table name.

Profit Margin

Now it's time to create the **Profit Margin** calculation (the profit margin is simply profit divided by sales). For this measure, you are going to use the `DIVIDE` function. The `DIVIDE` function is recommended over the divide operator (/) because the `DIVIDE` function automatically handles divide by zero occurrences. In the case of divide by zero occurrences, the `DIVIDE` function returns blank.

Create a new measure on the **Internet Sales** table using the following code:

```
Profit Margin = DIVIDE([Profit], [Total Sales])
```

Next, set the formatting as a percentage. From the modeling ribbon, click on the % icon, as shown in the following screenshot:

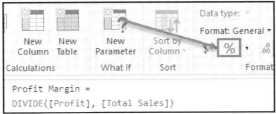

Figure 12-Setting formatting as a percentage

Optional parameters

You may have noticed that the DIVIDE function accepted three parameters and you only provided two. The third parameter allows you to set an alternative result for divide by zero occurrences. This alternate result is optional. Optional parameters are denoted by square brackets on both sides of the parameter. These optional parameters are prevalent in many DAX functions. Take a look at the following screenshot:

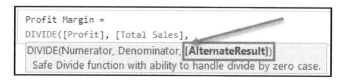

Figure 13-Optional parameters in DAX functions

Filter context

The automatic filtering that occurs in Power BI is a really awesome feature, and is one of the reasons that so many companies are gravitating to this tool. Automatic filtering is directly tied to the concept of the filter context. You were introduced to the filter context in the previous chapter. I want to briefly expand on the previous chapter here before discussing the **CALCULATE** function.

A simple definition of the filter context would be that it is simply anything in your report that is filtering a measure. There are quite a few items that make up the filter context. Let's take a look at a few of them:

- Any attributes in the rows; this includes the different axes in charts
- Any attributes in the columns
- Any filters applied by slicers (visual filters); slicers are discussed in the next chapter
- Any filters applied explicitly through the **Filters** pane
- Any filters explicitly added to the calculated measure

Calculate

The CALCULATE function is an extremely powerful tool in the arsenal of any DAX author. This is because the CALCULATE function can be used to ignore, overwrite, or change the existing filter context. You may be asking yourself why—why would anyone want to ignore the default behavior of Power BI? Let's take a look at an example.

Let's assume you want to return the total sales of each country as a percentage of all countries. This is a very basic percent of total calculation: **Total Sales** per country divided by **Total Sales** for all countries. However, how do you get the total sales of all the countries so that you can perform this calculation? This is where the CALCULATE function comes into the picture. Take a look at the following screenshot:

Sales Territory Country	Total Sales	Total Sales all Countries
Australia	9,061,000.58	29,358,677
Canada	1,977,844.86	29,358,677
France	2,644,017.71	29,358,677
Germany	2,894,312.34	29,358,677
United Kingdom	3,391,712.21	29,358,677
United States	9,389,789.51	29,358,677
Total	**29,358,677.22**	

Figure14-Calculating total sales of all the countries

To do the percent of total calculation, you need to get **Total Sales all Countries** on the same row as Total Sales. This means you need to create a new calculated measure that ignores any filters that come from the country attribute. Create a new calculated measure on your **Internet Sales** table using the following DAX formula:

```
Total Sales all Countries =
CALCULATE(
    [Total Sales],
    ALL(
        'Sales Territory'[Sales Territory Country]))
```

Figure 15-Create a new calculated measure on Internet sales table using DAX formula

The preceding calculation will return all sales for all countries, explicitly ignoring any filters that come from the **Country** column. Let's briefly discuss why this works.

The first parameter of the CALCULATE function is an expression, and you can think of this as an aggregation of some kind. In this example, the aggregation is simply Total Sales. The second parameter is a filter that allows the current filter context to be modified in some way. In the preceding example, the filter context is modified by *ignoring any filters* that come from the country attribute. Let's take a look at the definition for the **ALL** function used in the second parameter of the CALCULATE function:

ALL: Returns all the rows in a table, or all the values in a column, *ignoring any filters* that may have been applied.

Percentage of total calculation

Now, create another calculated measure on the **Internet Sales** table using the following code. Make sure that you format the measure as a percentage:

```
% of All Countries = DIVIDE([Total Sales], [Total Sales all
Countries])
```

In the following screenshot, you can see the completed example with both of the new measures created in this section. Without a basic understanding of the CALCULATE function, this type of percent of total calculation would be nearly impossible:

Sales Territory Country	Total Sales	Total Sales all Countries	% of All Countries
Australia	9,061,000.58	$29,358,677.22	30.86%
Canada	1,977,844.86	$29,358,677.22	6.74%
France	2,644,017.71	$29,358,677.22	9.01%
Germany	2,894,312.34	$29,358,677.22	9.86%
NA		$29,358,677.22	
United Kingdom	3,391,712.21	$29,358,677.22	11.55%
United States	9,389,789.51	$29,358,677.22	31.98%
Total	**29,358,677.22**	**$29,358,677.22**	**100.00%**

Figure 16- Completed example with both of the new measures

Time intelligence

Another advantage of Power BI is how easily time intelligence can be added to your data model. Within **data analysis expressions (DAX)**, you have a comprehensive list of built-in time intelligence functions to make this very easy. In this section, you are going to use these built-in functions to create the following measures:

- Year to Date Sales
- Year to Date Sales (Fiscal Calendar)
- Prior Year Sales

 Built-in time intelligence calculations do not work if you are using a direct query connection to your data source rather than importing data. Take a look at the alternative methods for calculating time intelligence in the DAX cheatsheet at https://tinyurl.com/pbiqs-daxcheatsheet.

Year to Date Sales

Create a new calculated measure on your **Internet Sales** table using the following DAX formula. Remember to format the measure as **$ English (United States)**:

```
YTD Sales = TOTALYTD([Total Sales], 'Date (Order)'[Date])
```

YTD Sales (Fiscal Calendar)

Maybe your requirement is slightly more complex, and you need to see the year-to-date sales based on your fiscal year end rather than the calendar year end date. The TOTALYTD function has an optional parameter that allows you to change the default year end date from "12/31" to a different date. Create a new calculated measure on your **Internet Sales** table using the following DAX formula:

```
Fiscal YTD Sales = TOTALYTD([Total Sales], 'Date (Order)'[Date], "03/31")
```

Now, let's take a look at both of these new measures in a table in Power BI:

Year	English Month Name	Total Sales	YTD Sales	Fiscal YTD Sales
2005	July	473,388.16	$473,388	$473,388
2005	August	506,191.69	$979,580	$979,580
2005	September	473,943.03	$1,453,523	$1,453,523
2005	October	513,329.47	$1,966,852	$1,966,852
2005	November	543,993.41	$2,510,846	$2,510,846
2005	December	755,527.89	$3,266,374	$3,266,374
2006	January	596,746.56	$596,747	$3,863,120
2006	February	550,816.69	$1,147,563	$4,413,937
2006	March	644,135.20	$1,791,698	$5,058,072
2006	April	663,692.29	$2,455,391	$663,692
2006	May	673,556.20	$3,128,947	$1,337,248
Total		**29,358,677.22**		

Figure 17-Both the new measure in a table

The newly created measures **YTD Sales** and **Fiscal YTD Sales** have both been added to the preceding table. Let's take a closer look at how these two measures are different; the relevant sections in the table are annotated with the numbers one to four, corresponding to the following notes:

1. The amount displayed for December 2005 is $3,266,374. This is the cumulative total of all sales from January 1, 2005 to December, 2005.

2. As expected, the cumulative total starts over as the year switches from 2005 to 2006; therefore, the YTD Sales amount for January 2006 is $596,747.

3. In the **Fiscal YTD Sales** column, the cumulative total works slightly differently. The displayed amount of $5,058,072 is the cumulative total of all sales from April 1st, 2005 to March 31, 2006.

4. Unlike the YTD Sales measure, the Fiscal YTD Sales measure does not start over until April 1. The amount displayed for April 2006 of $663,692 is the cumulative total for April. This number will grow each month until May 31, at which point the number will reset again.

Prior Year Sales

A lot of time series analysis consists of comparing current metrics to the previous month or previous year. There are many functions in DAX that work in conjunction with the CALCULATE function to make these types of calculations easy. You are going to create a new measure to return the total sales for the prior year.

Create a new calculated measure on your **Internet Sales** table using the following DAX formula:

```
Prior Year Sales =
CALCULATE(
    [Total Sales],          // SUM('Internet Sales'[Sales Amount])
    SAMEPERIODLASTYEAR(     // Change the filter context to go back one year
        'Date (Order)'[Date]))
```

Figure 18-Create a new calculated measure on your Internet sales

CALCULATE allows you to ignore or even change the current filter context. In the preceding formula, CALCULATE is used to take the current filter context and change it to one year ago. This calculated measure also works at the day, month, quarter, and year level of the hierarchy. For example, if you are looking at sales for June 15, 2018, then the **Prior Year Sales** measure would return sales for June 15, 2017. However, if you were simply analyzing your sales aggregated at the month level for June 2018, then the measure would return the sales for June 2017.

> For a comprehensive list of all the built-in time intelligence functions, please take a look at `https://tinyurl.com/pbiqs-timeintelligence`.

Summary

In this chapter, you learned that DAX allows you to significantly enhance your data model by improving the analytical capabilities with a relatively small amount of code. You also learned how to create calculated columns and measures and how to use DAX to perform useful time series analysis on your data. This chapter merely scratched the surface of what is possible with DAX. As you further explore the DAX language on your own, you will quickly become a proficient author of DAX formulas. As with everyone who learns DAX, you will inevitably learn that there is a layer of complexity to DAX that will require further education to really master. When you get to this point, it would be advantageous to look for classes or books that will help you to truly master DAX!

5
Visualizing Data

Up to this point, you have spent some time importing data and modeling it to your specifications. In this chapter, we will take that hard work and begin to visualize the data in efficient and effective ways. The most common association with Power BI for consumers is the ability to create very impactful visualizations of data, and there are many options available to do this. In this chapter, we will look at all the various options that are available to you within the Power BI Desktop application. Additionally, we will take a brief glimpse at the additional visualization options that are available through the Custom Visuals Marketplace. The topics detailed in this chapter are as follows:

- Data visualization basics
- Visuals for filtering
- Visualizing tabular data
- Visualizing categorical data
- Visualizing trend data
- Visualizing KPI data
- Visualizing geographical data
- Leveraging Power BI custom visuals
- Data visualization tips and tricks

At the time of this book's publication, there are 30 readily available visuals in the Power BI Desktop application; this includes the Shape map visual that is in the preview options. We will be exploring most of them and how they best work with certain types of data sets to bring the model we have worked on until this point to life!

With Power BI's rapid update cycle, there will be many visuals added to the application over time. If you would like to leverage these as soon as they are available, you can find them in the **Preview** section of the application's options. *Figure 5-1* shows how to access the **Preview Features** area. Once you have enabled something in this area, it usually requires you to restart the Power BI application, so make sure to save your work! The path is File||Options and Settings||Options||Preview Features.

How to turn on **Preview Features** can be seen here:

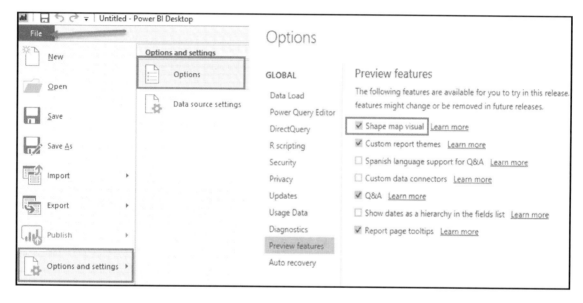

Figure 5-1

Data visualization basics

As soon as you launch the Power BI desktop application and close out of the initial splash screen, you will find yourself in the Report View, which is where we will stay for the duration of this chapter. In the previous chapter, you explored the Relationship view as well as the Data view, but these areas are not necessary for the visualization work we will be doing. There are many items of interest in this initial Report view area that we need to discuss so that we can work efficiently. Let's open the completed Power BI file from Chapter 4, *Leveraging DAX*, which includes all of the calculated columns and calculated measures that we will use in the upcoming visuals.

Let's review the key items from *Figure 5-2*:

For this chapter, you can build on top of the completed PBIX file from `Chapter 4`, *Leveraging DAX*. If you would like to keep your work from each chapter separate, please follow the noted steps here. Open the completed PBIX file called `Chapter 5`, *Visualizing Data*. Then, under the File option, choose Save As and give this file a new name for the work we will be doing in `Chapter 5`, *Visualizing Data*.

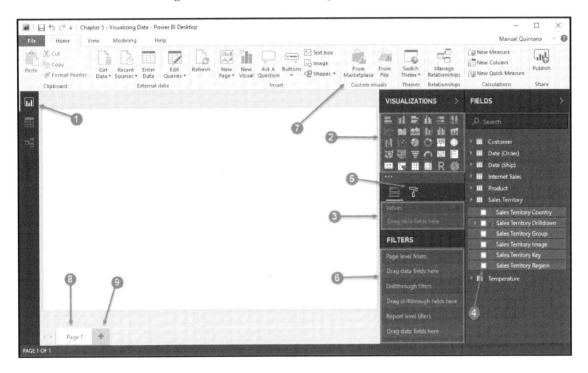

Figure 5-2

1. **Report view**: This is the button that will place us in the Report canvas and allow us to create visuals.
2. **Visuals area**: This is where we can choose which visual, we would like to use. Once custom visuals are added, they will appear here as well.

3. **Field area**: This area will change depending on the visual but it is where we place the fields we will use within the selected visual.

4. **Field pane**: These are all the available fields we have to choose from to add to our visuals.

5. **Format area**: Here is where we can decide on many things specific to either the entire report page or the selected visual, such as text size, font style, titles, and so on.

6. **Filters area**: This is where we can apply filters of various scopes:
    - **Page-level filters**: Any filters applied here will affect every single visual on the selected page.
    - **Drillthrough filters**: This option allows users to pass a filter value from a different report page to this one. This will be discussed in further detail in `Chapter 6`, *Digital Storytelling with Power BI*.
    - **Report-level filters**: Filters applied here will affect every single visual for the entire Power BI report.
    - **Visual-level filters**: This category will only appear when you have a visual selected, and the applied filters will only affect the selected visual.

7. **Custom visuals**: By selecting this button, you will have a menu appear that has access to all the custom visuals from the Microsoft store. You can then add whichever visual you would like to the Visuals area.

8. **Report page**: Here is where you can select which report page you would like to work with. Each page has a limited work area where we can use visuals, so it is common to have more than one page in a Power BI report.

9. **Add Report page**: By selecting this symbol, you can add a new report page to add more area in which we can add visuals.

It is important to note that when working with Visual level filters, the Fields area, and the Format area, you must have the specific visual selected. You can verify this when you see the various anchor points around the visual in question. Now that we have familiarized ourselves with the Report page features and layout, its time to start visualizing!

Visuals for filtering

Filtering the data that users will see within a Power BI report is the most effective way to answer very specific questions about that data, and there are many ways to accomplish this. One of Power BI's best features is its default capability to allow users to interact with a visual, which will then apply that as a filter to the rest of the visuals on that page, and this is known as interactive filtering. This behavior really puts the power into the users hands, and they can decide how they want to filter the visuals. This now makes a report so much more robust because it can answer so many more questions about the data. Along with this functionality, we, report developers, can add more explicit forms of filtering using the Slicer visual that is available to us in the visuals area. This allows us to choose a very specific field from our data, that we know our end users will want to manipulate to see that data in various different states. So now, lets dive in and get a better understanding on these two filtering options, as they will most definitely be elements we will see in our finished reports.

Interactive filtering

Almost every single visual that is readily available to us within Power BI has some sort of element that users can interact with. At the same time, every visual can be impacted by these very same elements. This really gives us a lot of room when it comes to deciding which visuals we would like in a report page. We will cover Interactive filtering again later on in this chapter, but it is important to understand how this feature works so that we can leverage it throughout the following examples. Let's create two very simple visuals based off our current data model so we can see exactly how this interactive filtering works. For right now, let's not worry about the details of these visuals as they will be fully described in later sections of this chapter.

Let's look at, setting up the example:

1. Select the **Stacked Column Chart** visual that will appear in the report canvas. Make sure you can see the anchor points we talked about earlier so that the following steps will work.
2. Now, let's add a couple of fields to the visual. In the Fields pane under the Internet Sales table, choose the **Total Sales** calculated measure by placing a check in the box to the left. You will notice that the field shows up under the **Value** section of the Field area.

3. Do the same thing for the **Sales Territory Country** field located under the **Sales Territory** table. This time, the field shows up under the **Axis** section of the **Field** area. Reference figure 5-3 here to validate that everything is set correctly:

Figure 5-3

You may notice that some of the visual elements do not meet your standards. For example, the size of the text for various items in this visual are far too small to read. These are the types of changes that we would make in the Format area but will not be doing in this specific example. We will be examining the most common Format changes for each of the visuals within their respective section in this chapter. Right now, we just want to see how interactive filtering works.

4. We can already start to interact with any of the columns we currently have, but since this is the only visual it really isn't that exciting. So, let's add another visual to the report canvas; make sure you left-click somewhere in the empty space so that no visual is currently selected.

5. Now, we can select the Pie Chart visual, which will be added to the report canvas. You may have to move the visual to a location more to your liking.

6. We will now add two fields to this visual, and the first will be the **Age Breakdown** calculated column. We can either place a check in the box next to the field, or we can drag that field on top of the correct visual; both methods will have the same affect and we should see the **Age Breakdown** field located under the **Legend** section.

7. Using either of the two methods just described, let's add the **Profit** calculated measure to this visual as well, which should populate under the **Values** section. See figure 5-4 to verify the setup. Remember, don't worry about formatting right now:

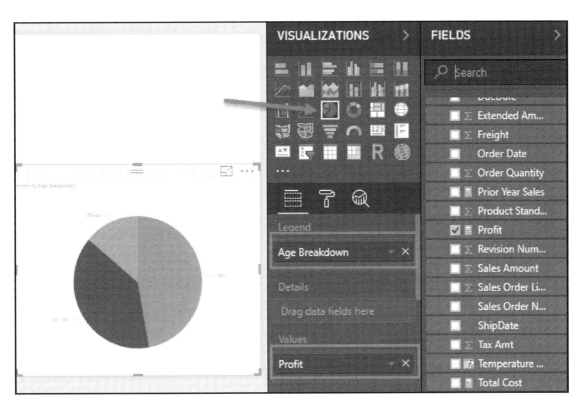

Figure 5-4

Now that the example is all set and there are two visuals in the report canvas, we can really see how interactive filtering works. Go ahead and select (left-mouse-click) the column labeled **United States** in the stacked column chart. You will immediately see that the pie chart changes to having a much smaller highlighted area. By hovering over the *35-44* section of the pie chart, we can now see that the United Stats makes up $413,617.35 of the $1,661,776.43 total for that category. This same type of filtering can be done by the pie chart, which will then affect the stacked column chart. Just with this simple example, you can see how effective interactive filtering is in answering questions about our data. Keep this in mind as we move forward with our other examples so you can keep seeing the impact this filtering has. We will cover additional option settings around interactive filtering at the end of this chapter.

The Slicer visual

So now that we know that interactive filtering will always be an option for users, what do we do when our end users want to filter by something that isn't used inside our visuals? This is where the **Slicer** visual comes into play. The **Slicer** visual only allows one field to be assigned to it but, depending on what data type that field is, we will have different presentation options. The first option will be if we wanted to use a field of a **String/Text** date type. The second option will appear if we use any of the **Numeric** data types, which include: **Decimal Number**, **Fixed Decimal Number**, **Whole Number** and any of the **Date** data types. This second option is referred to as a **Numeric Range Slicer**. Let's take a look at these two different options with the visuals we already have.

Let's look at, setting up the visual:

1. Select the **Slicer** visual and move it to some place convenient within the report canvas. You can use the anchor points to resize the visual as you see fit.
2. In our first example, let's add in the **Temperature Range** field from the **Temperature** table to our selected **Slicer** visual.

What we are seeing within our slicer is known as the List view. This allows users to see a distinct list of all the options they can now filter on from that specific field. For us, we can see that we now have four temperature options to choose from, and we can either single-select from our list, or multi-select. By simply left-clicking any of the boxes next to our options, we can see that both of our visuals become filtered based on the selected criteria. So, if we were to select the **Cold** option, the stacked column chart would be showing the Total Sales by Country when the weather was cold; see *Figure 5-5*:

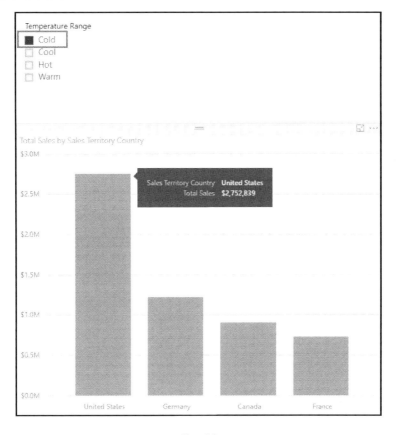

Figure 5-5

 In order to multi-select, you have two options. The first is to hold down the *Ctrl* key on your keyboard while making your selections. The second option lies within the *Format* area under the *Selection Controls* expandable menu. Here, you will find an option called *Single Select*, which is set to *On* by default, and by turning this off you no longer need to hold the *Ctrl* key to multi-select.

Now, let's add another slicer to our current report page, which uses a field of a numeric data type, so we can explore the *Numeric Range Slicer* .

Let's look at, setting up the visual:

1. Ensure that you have no other visual selected, and choose the **Slicer** visual once again. Resize and move the slicer to your liking.
2. For this slicer, let's add the `Year` field from the `Date (Order)` table.

Immediately, you will see a very different presentation for our filter options. We have a sliding bar that can be moved from either side to give us a range of values, which will be used to filter the other visuals on our page. By moving the left slider one value to the right, we can see that the year 2005 has now been removed from our range and the data in our visuals has changed; see *Figure 5-6*. It should be noted that this slicer that we are using to filter by year could also be set to use the **List** format that our temperature slicer is using. Imagine, though, if rather than choosing the **Year** field as we did, we selected the **Date** field. The **Date** field has so many unique choices for filtering that using the **List** format would be impossible. This is really where the range format for the slicer makes the most sense. As well, there are a couple other formats available to us within the slicer. We can find those options in the upper right-hand corner of the slicer visual. Let's take a look at what those formats are and when they are available to us:

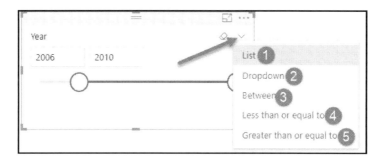

Figure 5-6

Format options from figure 5-6 are as follows:

1. **List**: This option is available no matter what field you select. It is a distinct list of values from the selected field. This is better used when there is a small amount of options to choose from.

2. **Dropdown**: This give the user a drop-down menu that will contain a distinct list of values from the selected field. This is very similar to the List option, but our choices are hidden until we hit the dropdown option. This is still meant for a smaller set of values so that users don't have to scroll through hundreds of choices.

3. **Between**: Here we have the option from our second example using the *Year* field. This choice will only present itself for fields that are of a numeric data type, and this includes dates. It allows users to specify a range of values to leverage as the filter by the use of a sliding bar.

4. **Less than or equal to**: Very similar to the Between option, but the sliding scale can only be adjusted from the left side.

5. **Greater than or equal to**: This is the same as the previous option, except you can only adjust the sliding scale from the right side.

When using the *List* option for a smaller set of filter choices, try changing the orientation from vertical to horizontal. If you add a background color to this setup, it gives the feeling of having buttons to filter with. To set this up, just go to the *Format* area of the slicer. Expand the *General* area and switch the value within the *Orientation* section to Horizontal. Then, expand the *Items* area and select a font color and background color of your choice, and you will see the design feels like a set of buttons.

So, now we know a couple different ways to allow our users to filter the visuals we have created for them. Interactive filtering will always be there for our users, but we can take a more traditional route with the *Slicer* visual and present them specific options they would find meaningful to filter the data. The last thing we will do is rename this report page from *Page 1* to *Slicers*.

Visualizing tabular data

We will see that there are many options within Power BI to visually represent data, but sometimes our users may want to see and compare detailed data and exact values. In these scenarios, using the *Table* or *Matrix* visual ends up being our best choice. When leveraging either of these two visuals, it is important to take advantage of the *Format* area to ensure that users can easily interpret the detailed data that is being presented. One of the best ways to bring attention to values of importance with these visuals is by using *Conditional Formatting*. We will explore this option, as well as take advantage of the hierarchies we created in `Chapter 3`, *Building the Data Model*, to allow for drill downs within the visuals.

The table visual

The table visual is perfect for looking at many values (measures) for a category. To really make the table shine, we will also want to take advantage of the *Conditional Formatting* option that is available to us. In our example, we will be using the *Sales Territory Region* as our category and looking at four different values for it.

Let's look at, setting up the visual:

1. Rename the blank page we are working on from `Page 1` to `Tabular Data`.
2. Select the Table visual and resize it to take up a little less than half the report canvas. Notice, similar to the slicer, that there is only one area in which to populate fields, called `Values`.
3. The first field we will want to select will be `Sales Territory Region` from the `Sales Territory` table; this will be our category.
4. Next, navigate to the `Internet Sales` table and select the `Total Sales` measure. Also, select the `Profit`, `Total Cost`, and `Total Transactions` measures. See *Figure 5-7* for reference:

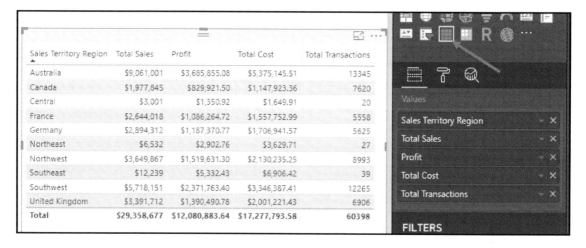

Figure 5-7

Already, we can see how this table provides great insights about our selected category, `Sales Territory Region`. By default, though, there are many formatting options that we will want to adjust. One of the first items will want to change is the size of the text for the data, as well as the headers. With the Table visual selected, go into the **Format** area (roller-brush icon) and expand the **Column Headers** section. We will see there are many options here for us, but for now let's simply adjust the *Text Size* option to something larger, making it easier to read the headers. Next, let's expand the *Values* area and make the same change here for the *Text Size* option. Now that our table is easier to read, let's explore the **Conditional Formatting** option, which will let us customize text or background colors based off values. If we return back to the **Fields** area where we can see our five options, you will note a small drop-down arrow next to each of our fields.

Select the arrow next to our `Total Sales` measure, and you will see the option for **Conditional Formatting,** as shown in *Figure 5-8.* When you place your mouse icon over the **Conditional Formatting** option, you will see that we are presented with three choices that are similar in functionality and setup. The one we will focus on is the the **Background color scales** option, so go ahead and select that option. A menu will appear in which we will simply only change one option; place a check mark in the box that is in the bottom left that says **Diverging**. After hitting okay, we will now see that our *Total Sales* column is color-coded so that we can easily identify the regions that are good (green) and bad (red) performers. This is something that we can choose to apply to whichever columns we feel would benefit most from **Conditional Formatting,** but it is not necessarily required. With the use of this table visual, we can get a very quick and detailed understanding of performance for our `Sales Territory Region` category.

 It is important to also remember about Interactive Filtering with the table visual. Any of the rows that are present within the table can be selected, and will apply a filter to all other visuals on the same page.

Figure 5-8

The Matrix visual

Where a table does a great job of allowing users to consume tons of detailed data about a single category, the *Matrix* visual can accomplish this for more than one category. The *Matrix* visual allows users to not only select a category for the rows, but means we can also select a field to populate the columns as well, which allows us to see detailed data at a cross sections for two categories. *Conditional formatting* is also available for use within the *Matrix* visual, and is incorporated in the same fashion as we accomplished in the previous example. Other than *Conditional Formatting*, the *Matrix* visual can take advantage of established hierarchies to give users that capability of drilling down into more granular data. Many of the other visuals can also take advantage of hierarchies, but for tabular data the *Matrix* visual does a great job with this.

Let's look at, setting up the visual:

1. Ensure that you do not have any other visual selected, and choose the *Matrix* visual from the visual's area.

2. Firstly, we will populate the *Rows* area with our `Sales Territory Drilldown`, which you will find under the `Sales Territory` table. You will see that when we place a check mark next to the `Sales Territory Drilldown` option, it brings in three different fields, starting with `Sales Territory Group`.

3. Next, we will select what is known as a natural hierarchy which Power BI automatically creates from our `Date (Order)` table. Place a check mark next to the `Date` field, which will bring in the Year, Quarter, Month, and Day fields. If these fields do not automatically become populated in the *Columns* area, just drag them to that location. Now, we have our two categories with options to drill down to get more granular data.

4. Lastly, let's add two measures to the *Matrix* under the *Values* area. Select both the *Total Sales* and *Profit* measures. See *Figure 5-9* for reference. Move and resize the *Matrix* as you see fit:

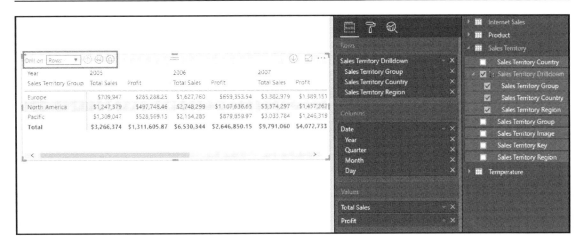

Figure 5-9

Now, we can see that the amount of data available to us is even greater than that of the *Table* visual. We should apply the same format changes to the *Text Size* as we did for the table at this point. The *Matrix* allows us to see fantastic detailed information about the different geographic regions, as well as a breakdown per year. Also, you will see that there are some new icons in the upper left of the visual which relate to the drilldown feature we spoke of earlier. Because we have hierarchies on both the rows and columns, we must decide which we would like to expand for further details. We will focus solely on the rows option and expand upon the geographical category. The first upward pointing arrow, which should be currently grayed out, allows users to move up a level in the hierarchy, but we are currently at the highest level. The option just to the right of this, which is depicted by two disconnected downward arrows, will change the category to the next level of the hierarchy, which is the *Sales Territory Country* in our example. Let's go ahead and select this option two times so that we are displaying the *Sales Territory Region*. The third option, which is depicted by two connected downward arrows will also go down one level at a time through the hierarchy, but it will also retain the previous (higher) category. By having the *Matrix* and *Table* next to each other, you can see the difference in detail that can be achieved by each of them. Both, though, can benefit greatly from *Conditional Formatting*.

Visualizing categorical data

Where the *Table* and *Matrix* visuals allow for a detailed look at multiple measures across a category, the following visuals are best for displaying data values across categories. In the upcoming visuals, we will be displaying Bars, Columns, and other visual elements, which will be proportional to the the data value. These visuals have a far less detailed few of the data, but it is very easy to distinguish the differences of the values within the chosen category. All of the visuals allow for interactive filtering and the use of drilldowns, which we will not focus on since it was covered in the previous examples. We will focus on how to understand and configure the following visuals:

- Bar and Column Charts
- Pie and Donut Charts
- The Treemap Visual
- Scatter Charts

We will continue using the same Power BI report from the previous examples, but we will want to create a new report page and call it *Categorical Data*.

Bar and Column charts

Both the *Bar* and *Column* charts are very similar in setup and how they visual data. The only difference here will be the orientation: the *Bar* chart uses rectangular bars horizontally where the length of the bar is proportional to the data, while the *Column* chart displays the bars vertically, but both are used to compare two or more values. Both of these visualizations have three different formats; *Stacked, Clustered,* and *100% Stacked.* For our example, we will focus on the *Bar* chart, but users can easily switch over to the *Column* just with the click of a button.

There are some situations where the *Bar* chart will better display data, and the same thing can be said of the *Column* chart. The biggest limitation for the *Column* chart would be the limited space on the *x*-axis where the category would go. So, if you have a lot of data labels or if they are very long, you may find that the *Bar* chart is the better option. An example where you might choose the *Column* chart over the *Bar* chart is if your data set contains negative values. In a *Bar* chart, the negative values will show on the left side while in a *Column* chart they will display on the bottom. Users generally associate negative values with a downward direction.

Let's look at, setting up the visual:

1. Select the *Stacked Bar Chart* option and move and resize the visual to take up a quarter of the report canvas.
2. The first field we will want to select is `Sales Territory Country`; this should populate in the *Axis* area.
3. Next, let's add our `Profit` measure, which should populate in the `Value` section.

Just with these two fields, we can very easily comprehend which countries make the most profit and which makes the least. As you can see though, there are more sections of the *Fields Area* that we can supply values for, namely the *Legend* section. By adding a category to this area, we can add sections to our original category, which shows the countries. Let's go ahead and add the *Age Breakdown* column to the legend for this visual (see *Figure 5-10*). Just like that, we have a very exciting display of our company's profit broken down by country and age group. Users can now hover over any section of the bar chart and the tooltip will display the values for that specific section. There is, though, another great format option that we can enable to make it even easier to understand the data, and it is called *Data Labels*. To enable this, simply select the *Format Area* and you will see an option called *Data Labels* that can be toggled on and off. By turning this option to *On*, we now can see the profit breakdown for each country by age category, as seen in *Figure 5-10*:

Figure 5-10

In regards to the other two options, *Clustered* and *100% Stacked*, you can simply select those visuals to experience the different presentations. You will notice the *Data Labels* remain and add great value regardless of the visual selection. As well with the addition of the *Legend*, we have another way to do interactive filtering.

Pie and Donut charts

Both the *Pie* chart and *Donut* chart are meant to visualize a particular section to the whole, rather than comparing individual values to each other. The only difference between the two is that the *Donut* chart has a hole in the middle, which could allow for some sort of label. Both of these visuals can be very effective in allowing interactive filtering, but if there are too many categories it can become difficult to read and interpret.

Let's look at, setting up the visual:

1. Ensure that no other visual is currently highlighted, and select the *Donut* chart visual. Move and resize the visual so as to take up a quarter of the report canvas, preferably above or below the *Bar* chart.
2. We will be populating two fields for this visual; the first will be *Temperature Range*, which should populate under the *Legend* section. The second field, which we want to show up in the *Values* section, is the *Total Sales* measure.

Because there are only four values within the *Temperature Range* category, this chart looks very clean and easy to understand. There is something, though, that we can add that will make it even easier to read: *Detail Labels*. This option is very similar to *Category Labels* in that we can display the data of each of the quadrants without having to use the tooltips. One thing that is different though is that it is already on, and all we need to do is decide how much detail we would like to have displayed. The more values that are present this can cause even more clutter though. To access these options go to the *Format Area* and expand the *Detail Labels* category, and manipulate the *Label Style* dropdown. For our example, let's choose the *All Detail Labels* option. As you can see in figure 5-11, we have a very nice and easy way to understand the presented data, as well as use it for interactive filtering:

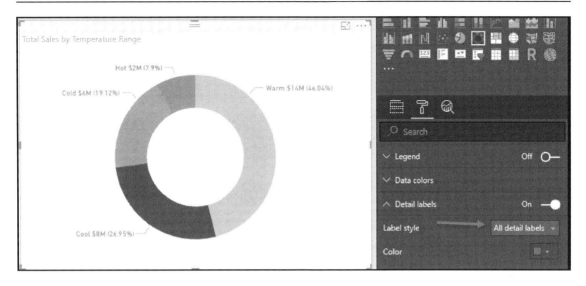

Figure 5-11

The Treemap visual

A fantastic visual for displaying hierarchies is definitely the *Treemap* visual. It accomplishes this by nesting the data in rectangles, which are represented by color, and this is commonly known as a "branch". If you add a category into the *Details* section of the visual you will note smaller rectangles within the "branches" and these are known as "leaves", hence the name *Treemap*. In order to really maximize this visual, we will need to do a little extra setup and bring in a new table, and create a new hierarchy. Let's go through this process now:

Let's look at, setting up the example:

1. We need to bring in the `DimGeography` table from the `AdventureWorksDW` excel workbook. Since we accomplished this during `Chapter 3`, *Building the Data Model*, you should be able to see this source under the *Recent Sources* option. If not, you can connect to this source by pointing to this location: `C:\Packt\Data Sources\AdventureWorksDW.xlsx`.

2. Once the *Navigator* appears, we will want to place a check mark next to the `DimGeography` table and hit **Load**.

3. We need to do a couple quick fixes to this new table before we can leverage it. Navigate to the Relationship View and delete the inactive relationship between `Sales Territory` and `DimGeography`.

4. Also let's rename this new table to `Geography` and hide the following fields: `FrenchCountryRegionName` and `SpanishCountryRegionName`.

5. Lastly, let's create a new hierarchy that we will use inside of this *Treemap* visual, as well as the Map visuals later on. Right-click on the `EnglishCountryRegionName` column and select New Hierarchy from the dropdown. Rename the new hierarchy `Region Drilldown`.

6. Add StateProvinceName to the hierarchy by right-clicking on it and selecting Add to Hierarchy from the dropdown. Repeat this step for the `City` field. See *Figure 5-12* for reference:

Figure 5-12

Now that we have a new geographical hierarchy that goes all the way down to a city level, we can see how this will display with our *Treemap* visual.

Let's look at, setting up the visual:

1. Click in any of the white space on the report canvas to ensure no visual is selected, and bring in the *Treemap* visual.

2. Move and resize this visual so that it takes up a quarter of the remaining report canvas.

3. First. we must decide on what we will be grouping on, and in our situation. that will be the newly defined `Region Drilldown`.

4. Next. we will add the `Total Sales` measure to the *Values* area and we start to see the beauty of this visual.

5. The last thing we will add is to the *Details* area so that we can see some "leaves". Bring in the `Year` field from the `Date (Order)` table.

The size of each of the rectangles is determined by the value being measured, which in our case is `Total Sales`. The "leaves" in this visual are portrayed by the `Year` category while our `Region Drilldown` creates the "branches". Because we are using a hierarchy, we have full access to the Drilldown capabilities shown earlier. You should also now be able to tell that the *Treemap* visual arranges the rectangles by size from top left (largest) to bottom right (smallest).

The Scatter chart

The last visual we will look at the is used for categorical data is the *Scatter* chart, sometimes referred to as the *Bubble* chart. This visual allows us to show the relationships between two or three numerical values. We are given the opportunity to place values for the x and y axis, but what is different about this visual is that we can add a third value for the size, and this is where the name *Bubble* chart comes from. There is also a very unique option available to us within the *Format Area* to really bring this data to life, and it is called the *Play Axis*. Let's go ahead and create our *Scatter* chart first, and then we will talk about the *Play Axis*.

Let's look at, setting up the visual:

1. Make sure no other visual is currently selected and choose the *Scatter* chart. Move and resize the visual to take up the remainder of the report canvas.

2. The first field we will select is the `Total Sales` measure, and this will serve as the value for our *X* axis.

3. For the *Y* axis, let us select the `Profit` measure.

4. The third value that we will use for the size of the bubbles will be the `Order Quantity` field.

5. Finally, we must choose the category that we would like to see all these measure for, and we will use the `EnglishCountryRegionName` field from the `Geography` table. Make sure that this field is displayed under the *Legend* section, which should give you a visual like in *Figure 5-13*:

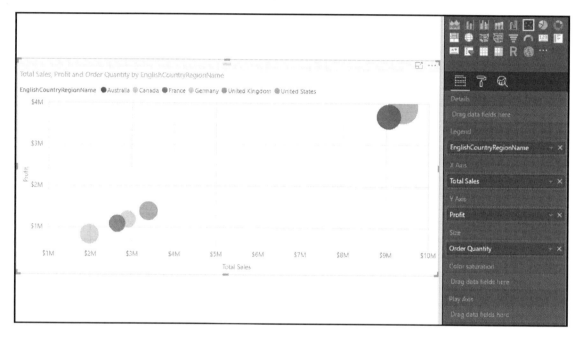

Figure 5-13

Now, the last part that we will add to this visual will be the *Play Axis*, which is unique to the *Scatter* chart. By adding some category of time, we can bring a little animation to this visual. For our example, let's add the *English Month Name* field to the *Play Axis* section, and you will see a *Play* button appear along with our 12 months. By hitting the button, you will now be able to watch the bubbles move to display their values at the specific moments in time.

Visualizing trend data

When we use the term *Trend Data,* we are talking about displaying and comparing values over time. Power BI gives us many options in this category, each with their own focus. The idea for each of the visuals, though, is to draw attention to the total value across a length of time. Let's create a new report page and call it *Trend Data,* and dive right in to see what the differences are between the following options:

- Line and Area Charts
- Combo Charts
- Ribbon Charts
- Waterfall and Funnel Charts

Line and Area charts

The *Line* chart is the most basic of our options when it comes to looking at data over time. The *Area* chart and *Stacked Area* chart are based on the line chart; the difference is that the area between the axis and the line is filled in with colors to show volume. Because of this, we will focus on the *Line* chart for our example. Since we have a very nice *Date* hierarchy, we will use this alongside a couple of measures to see trending.

Let's look at, setting up the visual:

1. Select the *Line* chart visual and move it to take up a qaurter of the report canvas.
2. The axis is where we dictate our time category and, for this example, we will use the built-in *Date* hierarchy by selecting the `Date` field from the `Date(Order)` table.
3. We will be using this chart to compare two different measures over time; they will be the `Total Sales` and `Prior Year Sales` measures. Select both of these, and they should populate under the `Values` section.

4. To make it a bit more of an exciting visual, let's take advantage of the hierarchy and it expand it down two levels to include the quarter and month, as seen in *Figure 5-14*:

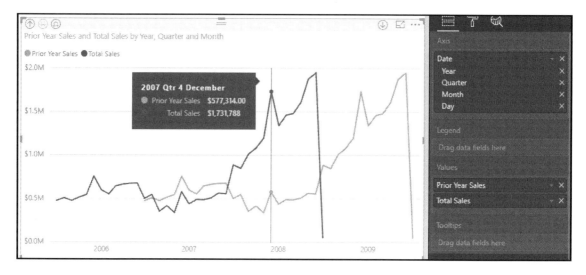

Figure 5-14

With this *Line* chart, we can clearly see there was a large growth in sales between 2007 and 2008. Visuals that focus on *Trend Data* can very easily illustrate any outliers, which can allow users to further investigate the cause for the seen trend. This visual can also benefit from some of the formatting options we have talked about previously, such as *Data Labels*.

Combo charts

As the name states, *Combo* charts combine the *Line* chart and *Column* chart together in one visual. Users can choose to have either the *Stack Column* format or the *Clustered Column* format. By combining these two visuals together, we can make a very quick comparison of the data. The main benefit of this type of chart is that we can have one or two *Y axes*. What this means is that we can either display two measures that would have the same Y axis, something like *Total Sales and Profit*. Or, we could show two measures that are based on completely different values such as *Order Quantity and Profit*; let's use the two for our example.

Let's look at, setting up the visual:

1. For this example, we will be using the *Line and Stacked Column Chart* visual. Select and resize it to take up a quarter of the report canvas.
2. For the *Shared Axis* area, let's select the Date field from the Date (Order) table.
3. We will then select the Order Quantity field to populate the *Column Values* section.
4. The last field we will select is the Profit measure, but when we check mark this item you will see that it is placed under the *Column Values* section, which is incorrect. Simply drag the *Profit* measure to the *Line Values* section.

In this example, you can see that we have two Y axes; the left one relates to the *Order Quantity* while the right one corresponds with our *Profit* measure. Go ahead and expand the hierarchy one level; this will give us more data points to see the trending between the two measures, as seen in *Figure 5-15*. From this visual, it's fairly easy to validate that when we sell more items we make more profit. This, like many other visuals, can also benefit from *Data Labels:*

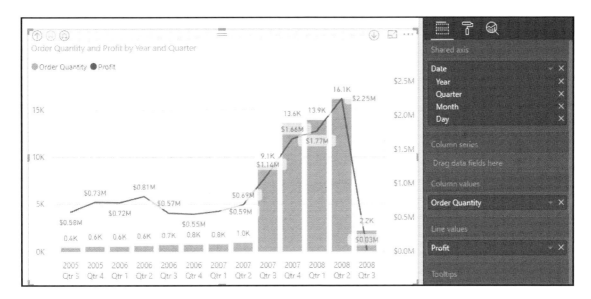

Figure 5-15

The Ribbon Chart

The *Ribbon Chart* is no different than the other visuals we just worked with; it is good at viewing data over time. What makes *Ribbon Charts* effective though is their ability at showing rank change; the highest range or value is always displayed on the top for each of the time periods. The chart also does have a unique visual flowing appeal to it that is different than the other visuals. Let's take a look that the *Ribbon Chart*.

Let's look at, setting up the visual:

1. Select the **Ribbon Chart** to add as a new visual, and resize it to take up a quarter of the report canvas.
2. For the *Axis* area, lets choose the *Date* field from the `Date (Order)` table so that we have a hierarchy available for drilldown.
3. The next field we will add to the visual is the *Total Sales* measure, which should populate under the *Value* section. At this point, you will see that it pretty much looks like a **Column Chart**.
4. Once we add a category to the *Legend* area, we will get that flowing ribbon presentation. For our example, lets add the `EnglishCountryRegionName` to the *Legend* area.

The first thing you may notice is the lighter areas between time periods; this is really one of the best parts of the **Ribbon Chart**. This area shows the value for the category for the previous period and the upcoming one. Also, the tooltip does give each value a rank and shows any increases as well as decreases. This, like many other visuals, also gets a nice visibility bump by adding *Data Labels*, as seen in *Figure 5-16*:

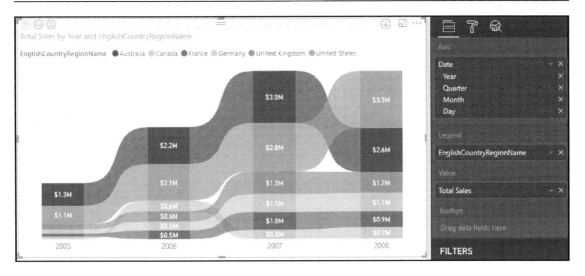

Figure 5-16

The Waterfall Chart

This next visual, the *Waterfall Chart*, is very helpful in understanding the changes that occur from an initial value. It displays a running total in relation to values being added or subtracted. By populating a field in the *Breakdown* option of the visual, we can see if it has had a positive or negative impact from value to value. Let's set up an example of the *Waterfall Chart*.

Let's look at, setting up the visual:

1. In our current report page we should have a quarter of the area still available. We will use half of this for the *Waterfall Chart*. Let's go ahead and now add this visual to the report page.

2. The first area we want to populate is `Category`, and for this we will select the `Date` field from the `Date (Order)` table. As before, this will bring in a hierarchy.

3. Next, select the `Profit` measure to represent the *Y axis*. With this, we can see how much each year has contributed to the total profit.

4. The last field we will select is `Age Breakdown`. Upon selecting this field, you will need to move it to populate the *Breakdown* section.

Now, we can see the strength of the *Waterfall Chart*, and we can see how much contribution each age group provided between years. By default, the visual uses the green color to indicate positive changes and red to illustrate negative ones, but this can be changed from the *Format Area* if you are so inclined. Depending on how many values are within your breakdown category, enabling *Data Labels* can be useful in this visual, as seen in *Figure 5-17*:

Figure 5-17

The Funnel Chart

The *Funnel Chart* allows users to see the percentage difference between values. Normally, the highest value is at the top and the lowest is at the bottom, which gives the look of a funnel. Each stage of the funnel with tell the percentage difference between itself and the previous stage, as well as compared to the highest stage. With this type of design, it makes sense that the *Funnel Chart* is very effective when visualizing a linear process with at least three or four stages. Our data set does not have a process with multiple stages, but we can still create something that gives us value.

Let's look at, setting up the visual:

1. With the remaining space we have on this report page, go ahead and add in the last visual for this section, the Funnel Chart.
2. For this visual, we will only be adding two fields. The first will be the `CountryRegionCode`, which will be what we use for the *Group* section.
3. The second item that we will add to the `Values` section will be the **Profit** measure.

The way we have set up this visual allows us to very easily identify which countries make the most profit and which make the least, but this is something we can achieve with many other visuals. What gives the *Funnel Chart* an edge is when we hover over one of the sections within the funnel and note the items that appear within the tooltip. You will see, when we hover over the section for France, that the tooltip lets us know how it compares to the section directly above it, as well as how it compares to the highest section, which is represented by the United States.

Visualizing KPI data

Key Performance Indicator is what KPI stands for. It is a measurable value that demonstrates how well a company is achieving a certain objective. With Power BI, we have a couple of options to measure the progress being made towards a goal for operational processes. The strength of a KPI visual lies in its simplicity. It displays a single value and its progress toward a specific goal. Let's create a new *Report Page* called *KPI Data*, and take a closer look at the *Gauge and KPI* visuals.

The Gauge visual

The *Gauge* visual displays a single value within a circular arc and its progress towards a goal or target value that we specify. The *Target Value* is represented by a line within the arc. With our current data set, we do not have a measure that we can use to illustrate an accurate business goal, so we will have to create it. Before we set up this visual, we will need to create a new calculated measure.

Let's look at, setting up the example:

1. We will be using the `Total Sales` measure as our value in the *Gauge* visual.
   Our target will be 10% more than the previous year's total sales, so we need to
   use DAX to create this measure.
2. Right-click the `Internet Sales` table and select the *New Measure* option, which
   would bring us to the formula bar.
3. Name the measure `Sales Target`, and use the following DAX formula to get
   our target:

```
Sales Target = [Prior Year Sales] * 0.1
```

Now that we have all the measures we need, lets set up the gauge visual and create our first
KPI.

Let's look at, setting up the visual:

1. Select the *Gauge* visual and move/resize it as you see fit.
2. For the **Value** section, select the `Total Sales` measure.
3. Select our newly created `Sales Target` measure for the `Target Value` area.
   Upon selecting this measure, it will not automatically be populated for the *Target
   Value*, so you will need to move it.

Using a *Slicer* visual alongside this KPI will be really helpful with our data set. Go ahead
and add the *Slicer* visual using the *Year* field for the value. If you choose the year 2008, you
will see that the value changes along with the target, as seen in *Figure 5-18*. With our data
set, the year 2008 is where we have our most recent transactions, and because of this visual,
we can see that we have still not met our goal. If you look at any of the other previous
years, we can validate that we were able to surpass our target every time:

Figure 5-18

The KPI visual

Where the *Gauge* visual uses the circular arc to show the current progress, the *KPI* visual takes a more explicit approach and just shows the value in plain text, along with the goal. The only real visual elements that are in play with this visual occur when the indicator value is lower than the goal and the text is shown in red, and when it has surpassed the goal and the text is in green. This is definitely one of the more direct visuals and perfectly exemplifies what we want for a KPI.

Let's look at, setting up the visual:

1. Ensure that no other visual is selected, and bring in the *KPI* visual, and move it as you see fit.
2. For the *Indicator* section, go ahead and select the `Total Sales` measure.
3. Next, choose the Prior Year Sales measure to represent the *Target Goals* section.
4. The last piece that we need to add is for the *Trend Axis,for* which we will be using the `Year` option from the `Date (Order)` table.

If, after following the preceding steps, the visual displays a value of *Blank* for the indicator, do not worry. This is because it is trying to show the total sales for the year 2010, the most recent value in our dataset. Unfortunately, we do not have any sales for 2009 or 2010, so to have this visual display correctly simply choose any other year from the slicer that we added in the previous section. Once you have accomplished this, you will now be able to view the *KPI* visual, and it should look like *Figure 5-19*:

Figure 5-19

Visualizing geographical data

One of the most exciting ways to visualize data in Power BI is through the various map options that we have. All the maps serve the same purpose to illustrate data in relation to locations around the world, but there are some small differences between each of them. All of the maps, except the *Shape Map,* have the option to provide the latitude and longitude coordinates, which will be the best way to ensure the appropriate location is being displayed. The reason for this is because the information that we provide the visual will be sent to *Bing Maps* to verify the positioning on the map. If we do not provide enough detail, then *Bing* may not return the desired results. For example, if we were to provide the map visual with a field that contains only the city name, that could result in some confusion because there may be multiple cities in the US with that name. In these scenarios, we will either want to supply some sort of geo-hierarchy to give better definition, or we can create new columns with more detailed information. Power BI also has a built-in feature when dealing with geographic data that allows users to help identify the type of data that is being provided: this is called *Data Category*. Let's go ahead and take advantage of this for our data set to make the map visuals more accurate.

Let's look at, setting up the example:

1. Within the **Fields** Pane, expand the Geography table.
2. The first field that we will categorize will be the City field. Highlight this field and then navigate to the **Modeling** ribbon. Once here, you will see the **Data Category** option.
3. Inside of the drop-down menu, we will select the City option. Upon accomplishing this, you will see that there is now a globe icon next to the City field.
4. Repeat the steps above for the StateProvinceName field, but choose the State or Province option for the data category dropdown.
5. The final field that we need to perform these steps for is EnglishCountryRegionName; select the Country/Region option from the dropdown.

Now that we have given a better description of our geographical data, we can proceed with using the various map visuals. One thing of note is that using any of these visuals does require internet access because we are going to be sending data to *Bing Maps*. Before we begin, create a new *Report Page* called Geographical Data.

The Map visual

The first visual we will use to illustrate geographical data is simply called the *Map* visual. This visual is also referred to as the *Bubble Map* because it plots the points of data with circles that can be set to change in size based off a supplied measure. With this visual, if you have the latitude and longitude coordinates in your data set, then nothing needs to be sent to *Bing Maps*. We do not have such detailed data, so we will need supply the necessary information through the *Location* section, which will be sent to *Bing Maps*.

Let's look at, setting up the visual:

1. For this new report page, lets select the *Map* visual to get things started, and move it to take up a quater of the report canvas.
2. To ensure there is no confusion about the locations we want to map, we will provide the geo-hierarchy, which we have created within the Geography table. Go to this table and select the Region Drilldown option, which will populate the **Location** section. Just with this, we can see the six countries represented by a bubble.

3. Next, we will add a measure that will dictate the size of the bubbles we are currently seeing. Let's use the `Total Sales` measure for the *Size* section, so that larger bubbles will show countries with higher sales amounts.

4. The last thing we will add to this visual is the Age Breakdown to the *Legend* section. With this, the bubbles start to look like little pie charts, as seen in *Figure 5-20*:

Figure 5-20

 When using a geo-hierarchy with a map, enabling the Drill Mode, which is signified by the down arrow in the upper right, can make this visual even more enjoyable. Remember this for any visual where we have a hierarchy selected; you should explore the different views it gives you.

The Filled Map visual

Unlike the traditional *Map* visual, which uses a bubble to indicate locations, the *Filled Map* visual uses shading to display the geographic data. So, the lighter an area looks, the lower the representative value. For this visual, it is recommended to visit the *Format Area* and dictate the range of colors for the shading so it will appear more apparent.

Let's look at, setting up the visual:

1. Select the *Filled Map* visual and move it to take up a quarter of the report page.
2. Just like the previous example, we will use the `Region Drilldown` from the `Geography` table to populate the *Location* section.
3. The only other field we will add to this visual is the *Profit* measure, which will control the *Color Saturation* option.

With just these setting, we can see the effect of this map, but because of the color selection it is very difficult to see the lighter shades; let's fix this. By going into the *Format Area* and expanding the *Data Colors* section, we will be presented with a couple of options. The first one we should turn on is the option labeled *Diverging*. Next, we should change the colors so that they are more distinguishable. For this example, lets use a more traditional option for our colors; red for M*inimum*, yellow for *Center*, and green for M*aximum.*

The Shape Map visual

Similar to the *Filled Map*, the *Shape Map* visual uses shading/saturation to show the geographic data. One thing that does make the *Shape Map* unique is that it allows users to upload their own maps to be illustrated. In order to accomplish this, you must have a JSON file which contains all the necessary information required by Power BI. By default, the visual does offer some standard maps but currently does not have an option to show the entire world. Let's take a look at the *Shape Map* visual.

Let's look at , setting up the visual:

1. Select the *Shape Map* visual and move it to take up a quarter of the report page.
2. This map does not allow for multiple fields to be placed in the *Location* section, so we cannot use the *Region Drilldown* as before. For this example, we will use the *StateProvinceName*. Do not be alarmed if nothing appears initially, as we still have to tell Power BI which map we want to use.
3. Before we go into the *Format Area* to choose a map, lets add the *Profit* measure, which will control the shading/saturation.
4. Now, we can look at the *Format Area* and expand the *Shape* option, where there will be a dropdown selection for the *Map* category. For our example, we will want to choose *USA: states*.
5. This is another example where taking control of what colors will be used for the shading can be helpful, so lets apply the same changes that we did for the *Filled Map* under the *Data Colors* section.

The ArcGIS Map visual

The final map we will talk about is the *ArcGIS Map* visual; this one is very different in that there is an option to pay for additional features. Also, the location where you can make visual changes to the map is different as well. Normally, we would access the *Format Area* but for this map you must hit the ellipsis in the upper-right corner of the visual and choose the *Edit* option. We will be focusing on a couple of areas here, but there are lots of options that are worth exploring. Let's take a look on how to configure the *ArcGIS Map* visual.

Let's look at, setting up the visual:

1. We should have one more section available within the report canvas to place this last visual, so lets select the *ArcGIS Map* visual.
2. Just like the *Shape Map* we are unable to select multiple fields to populate the *Location* section; we will use *StateProvinceNanme* for our example. You will notice that after loading the information there will be a small yellow ribbon at the bottom saying that it failed to load some of the information. This is fine, because this field contains provinces that are outside the United States.
3. The only other field that we will map for this visual will be the *Total Sales* measure, and we will use this for the *Color* section.

This visual is ready to go with the configuration that we have set, but if we want to change how things looks we must go a new route. In the upper right-hand corner you will see an ellipsis; left-click this and choose the *Edit* option. This brings us to a display that looks very similar to *Focus Mode,* but you will notice there are quite a few options at the top of the map. The first area we will visit to make a slight change will be the *Symbol Style* option. Here, we can control the level of transparency as well as the color palette being used. Select the dropdown menu for the *Color Ramp* option, and choose whatever selection you find enjoyable. This is the only change we will be making for our example, but you should take the time and examine all the other options available to you. Remember, there are even more options to choose from if you decided to subscribe and pay for this visual. All of these maps are very similar but each has a specific functionality that does not exist in the others. The traditional *Map* and *Filled Map* visuals are the most common ones used, but you will need to decide when one might illustrate your data set better than the other.

Leveraging Power BI custom visuals

Throughout this chapter, we have seen many different visuals and how they work with specific types of data. Although we already have many options readily available with Power BI, we have access to 100+ more visuals from the Microsoft store right at our fingertips. Users can either navigate to the Microsoft app store via any web browser, or while inside of the Power BI desktop application they can select the *From Marketplace* option in the home ribbon. Once you select this option, a menu will appear where you can simply search the entire collection of custom visuals available. Once you have found a visual that you would like to use, just hit the *Add* button shown in yellow. Users can also download the physical file as well, which can be uploaded into Power BI by using the *From File* option, which is also in the home ribbon. It is important to understand that when you select a custom visual, it saves as part of the Power BI report file and doesn't remain inside of the application. So, if you just downloaded a custom visual and then closed down Power BI, when you restart the application you will not see that custom visual unless you open the report you saved the custom visual to. This is a fantastic feature, and it only continues to grow so it is definitely worthwhile to check out the marketplace.

Data visualization tips and tricks

We have created six different report pages filled with different visuals and looked into different configuration options for each of them. That being said, we have barely scratched the surface of all the features that are available to us, and with the very quick update cycle Power BI has, that list of features will keep growing. In this final section, we will look at a couple of features that are not exclusive to just one visual, but can really help out when designing a report. It is highly recommended to watch the monthly videos that the Power BI team produces alongside the actual product update. This way, you can know exactly what is new and how to use it.

Edit interactions

Throughout all of our examples, we have had the capability of using interactive filtering. We know that almost everything we see inside a visual can be selected, and it will affect all the other visuals within that same report page. This behavior can be altered though, and there will be situations where you do not want a specific visual to be filtered by any others. The way we can control this is through an option called *Edit Interactions,* which can be found under the *Format* ribbon when a visual is selected. When you select the *Edit Interactions* button, you will see new icons for all of the other visuals that are currently not selected, as seen in figure 5-21. In this example, I have the *Pie Chart* selected and I can now decide if any of the other visuals will be affected by interactive filtering from the *Pie Chart.* The two primary icons are a funnel which lets us know that the visual will be filtered, and then a circle with a line through it designates that it will not be filtered. Occasionally, there will be an icon that looks like a pie chart chart, which we can see for the *Stacked Column Chart.* This means that the visual will be filtered by highlighting the filtered portion, as shown in *Figure 5-21.* This option is something that you will have to do for each individual visual:

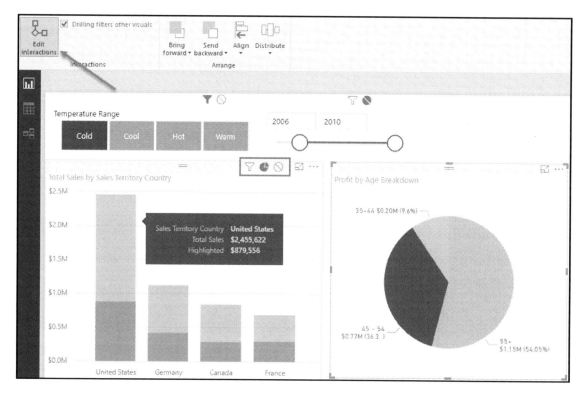

Figure 5-21

The Analytics pane

For every visual we worked with the *Field Area* and the *Format Area* but there is a option you may have noticed that is called the *Analytics Pane*. This option is available for most visuals, but some of the options will not appear; for our example we will look at the *Line Chart* example we created. Once we have that visual selected, we can choose the *Analytics Pane* and see that we are presented with seven different lines that can be added to the visual. All we have to do is decide which one we would like to be displayed and turn it on. For our visual, lets add an *Average Line* by expanding that section and selecting the *Add* option. Once the line has been added, we can change the color, name, transparency, style, and position from this same area, as seen in *Figure 5-22*. Users can add as many of these lines as they so choose, but remember, more is not necessarily better:

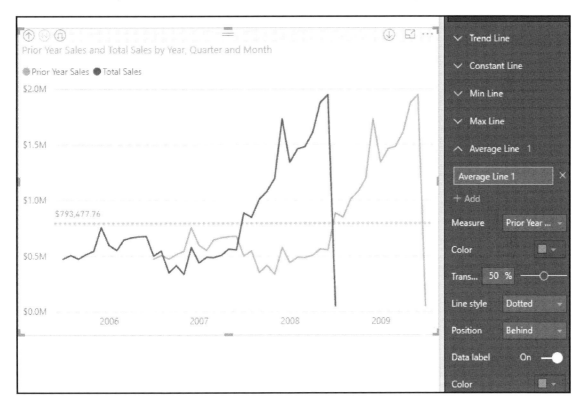

Figure 5-22

The Top N filter

At the very beginning of this chapter, we briefly talked about the *Filter Area* and how we can apply filters to different scopes. There are a couple choices available to users for the filter fields, but we are going to look at the *Top N* option. Even though it is called the *Top N* filter, this option allows us to create a filter that will show either the top or bottom number of values. For example, if we look at the *Ribbon Chart* we created, we can see that there are six countries that appear in the visual. With this filter, we can set it so that it only displays the top four countries based off a measure that we choose. So, in this situation, we could have that measure be `Total Sales`, which is what the visual is showing, or really anything we want. Lets go ahead and hit the dropdown next to the `EnglishCountryRegion` field in *Visual Level Filters*. If *Top N* isn't showing by default in the *Filter Type* section, go ahead and select it from the dropdown. For the *Show Items* section, we will leave the value of *Top* and manually input the number 4, as shown in *Figure 5-23*. The last thing that needs to be done is to decide what measure will be used to determine the top four countries; we will keep things simple and drag in the `Total Sales` measure, and hit **Apply Filter**. The most important thing to remember is that you can use any measure you want for this filter:

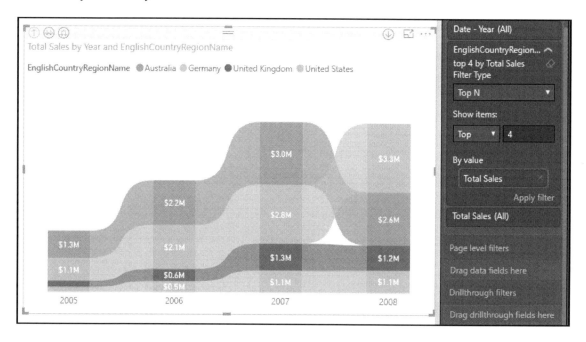

Figure 5-23

Show value as

Earlier in this chapter, we went through an example to take advantage of *Conditional Formatting*. This option can be found by hitting the downward arrow next to a field that is being used in a visual. Within this area is where we will find another option that is labeled *Show Value As*. This option will only be available for numeric data types, and allows us to show the values as a percentage of the grand total. The best way to take advantage of this is to place an identical column side by side and then use this option to display one of them as a percentage. For our example, lets revisit the *Matrix* visual we created for the *Tabular Data* section. Locate the `Profit` measure in the `Fields` Pane and drag it into the `Values` section for the visual, and place it directly after the `Profit` measure that we already had in place, referencing *Figure 5-24*. The visual looks a little odd since there is a duplicated column, but lets change it to show a percentage. Within the dropdown for the second representation of `Profit`, choose the **Show Value** As option and select **Percent of Grand Total**. The *Matrix* was already a great visual to quickly see a lot of metric information about the `Sales Territory Regions`, but now we have a firm understanding of what percentage each country is contributing to the grand total:

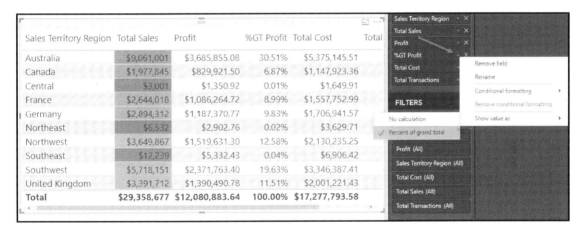

Figure 5-24

Summary

In this chapter, we focused on how to configure visuals and what data they best illustrate. We also saw a couple of the most common formatting options that are used with these visuals. In the next chapter, we will look into the concept of digital storytelling. Power BI has a strong set of options that we can leverage to allow users to experience and navigate through the data in an adventurous and exploratory manner.

Digital Storytelling with Power BI

6

In the previous chapter, you learned how to explore many of the readily available visuals within Power BI and saw how they can showcase our data. With the assistance of interactive filtering, we can also make it so that the visuals can work with each other. But there is so much more than just simple drag-and-drop reporting within Power BI. I'm referring to its storytelling features. Alongside all of the different visuals, Power BI has a set of features that can tie together not only individual charts and graphs, but that can also allow users to navigate through multiple pages to discover exactly what they want from the data. Using these features, we can weave together our data in a way that allows for interactivity far beyond what we have already seen. This really allows users to take control of how they will view your Power BI report. If they just want to take a quick glance at a summary view of the data, they can, but if they wish to dive deeper, we can grant them multiple paths to take. In this chapter, we will look into the following digital storytelling features:

- Configuring Drillthrough filters
- Storytelling with the Selection pane and bookmarks

When using these features, there are many different approaches that can be taken. We will be looking at them in their most basic forms, but they can flourish when you use your imagination. At the time of this book's publication, the idea of digital storytelling has become extremely popular, and will more than likely foster even more features for the future of Power BI, so keep an eye out!

For this chapter, we will be using the completed Power BI file from `Chapter 5`, *Visualizing Data*. If you have not completed this on your own, you can open a completed version, located at `C:\Packt\Completed Examples\Chapter 5 - Visualizing Data Completed.pbix`. It is recommended that, upon opening this file, you immediately use the **Save As** option and name the report `Chapter 6 - Digital Storytelling`. By doing this, you can preserve your work from chapter to chapter.

Configuring drillthrough filters

As we have seen with Power BI, we are limited to the space that is given to us within each report page, so we have to make the most of what we are given. Until now, that is. The main purpose of the *drillthrough* feature is to allow communication between two pages in your Power BI report. You can now create a page within your report that focuses on something very specific and detailed that you might have left out because there wasn't enough room on the page that had visuals relating to this data. Now you can use drillthough filters on that focused page, and your users can right-click on any data point on any other report page and they will be taken to the focused report, which will be filtered by whatever context was in that selected data point. Also, when we set up the drillthrough filters, we have two options. The first option is to set the focused page to only be filtered by specific filters; all other filters that are part of the selected data point when drilling through will be ignored if they are not specified. The second option is where we allow all filters that are part of the selected data point to filter the focused page; this option is known as **Keep all filters**, and can be toggled **On** or **Off**, as seen in *Figure 6.1*:

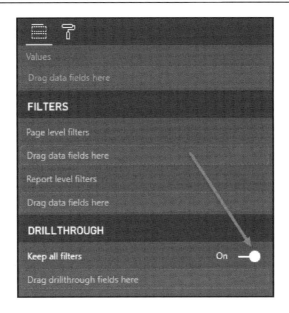

Figure 6.1

For our example, we will be setting the **Keep all filters** option to **On**. Let's go ahead and set up the example by copying some of the visuals we created previously in Chapter 5, *Visualizing Data,* and then moving them into new pages, where we will leverage the drillthrough filter option.

Let's look at, setting up the example:

1. Create two new report pages: the first one should be called **Summary Page** and the second should be **Drillthrough Page**.
2. Select the **Summary Page** report page and add a **Stacked Column Chart** visual. Resize the visual to take up half of one side of the page.
3. The first field we will select to populate the visual will be our **Profit** measure, which should be placed under the **Value** section.
4. Next we will fill the **Axis** section with our **Region Drilldown** to bring in the three geographic fields.

5. Lastly, select the **Year** field from the **Date (Order)** table to represent our **Legend**. See *Figure 6.2* for reference:

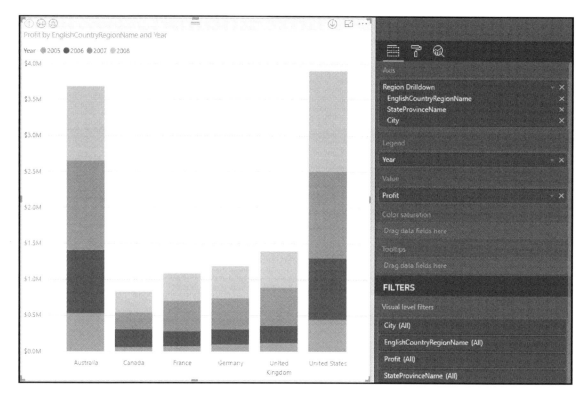

Figure 6.2

6. Now let's create that focused page by adding visuals to the **Drillthrough Page**. The first visual we will add is a **Table** visual. Resize the visual to take up a third of the report page, but leave a small amount of space above the visual.

7. Select the following fields in the order given: **StateProvinceName** | **City** | **Year** (from the **Date (Order)** table) | **Profit**.

8. Now add in another visual. Select the **Map** visual to take up the other two thirds of the report page.

9. In the **Location** section, choose the **City** field and place the **Profit** measure under the **Size** section.

10. Now we will use the **Drillthough filter** option. Select and drag the **EnglishCountryRegionName** field into the **Drillthrough** section.

Upon placing a field into the **Drillthrough** area, you will notice that an image is automatically added to the page in the upper left-hand corner. This is simply an image that has been set with an action to go "back" to the previous page. By selecting the image, you will find that there are quite a few familiar format settings available in the **Format Area**. One of more common settings to change is the **Fill** option, which will allow the selection of a color to make the "Back" arrow more visible. Everything is set for the example, so now we can see how the **Drillthough** option works. Navigate back to the **Summary Page** and right-click the **2008** (Yellow) section for **United States**. You will see that there is now an option called **Drillthrough**, and when you hover the mouse over this new option, you will be presented with a list of available **Drillthrough** reports. In our scenario, we only have one option, but it is important to note that you can have as many drillthough reports as you desire. Upon left-clicking the **Drillthough Page** option, you will be taken to that page, and you will see that both visuals have been filtered by the values of **United States** and **2008**. If we were to go back to the **Summary Page** and make a different selection, those new filters would take effect on these two visuals. Thus, we can see that now we have two report pages that interact with each other. As more and more pages are added to our report, users will always have the option to drillthough to this report with whatever filters they have chosen.

Storytelling with the Selection pane and bookmarks

Interactive filtering and drillthrough filters really have a a big impact on how users consume the data in our Power BI reports. Sometimes, though, we may want to ensure that our users see the data in a very specific way that will truly show its impact. We can guide report consumers in a very interactive way by using bookmarks as well as the **Selection** pane. Using these options, we can make better use of the available space that is given to us for each report page and still make it feel as if users have a lot of choices as to how they will view the data.

Bookmarks pane

The bookmark features allow report creators to capture the view of a report page. This includes the filtering and the state of the visuals at the time when the bookmark was created, allowing them to return to that state by simply selecting the bookmark in question. There are some additional options that we will explore a little later on, but lets begin with the basics on to use this storytelling feature. To gain access to the bookmarks, simply access the **View** ribbon and place a check mark next to the **Bookmarks Pane** option. You will see a new window present itself next to the **Visualizations** pane. Because we have not created any bookmarks, the only option we have is to **Add**, but first, we need to bring in a couple more visuals to the **Summary Page** to make it worthwhile.

Let's take a look at, setting up the example:

1. Select the **Trend Data** report page and highlight the **Line Chart**, which showcases the **Total Sales** and **Prior Year Sales** measures from the years 2005–2009. What we want to do is copy this visual directly over to the **Summary Page**. This can be done by holding the *Ctrl + C* keys on the keyboard. If this is not possibly, simply take note of the settings for this visual and recreate it on the **Summary Page**.

2. Next, let's add a slicer to the **Summary Page** using the **Age Breakdown** field for the values. To make this look a bit nicer, let's make this slicer look like a button by visiting the **Format Area** for the slicer and changing the **Orientation** selection to **Horizontal** with the **General** dropdown. You can also change the coloring to your liking, as shown in *Figure 6.3*:

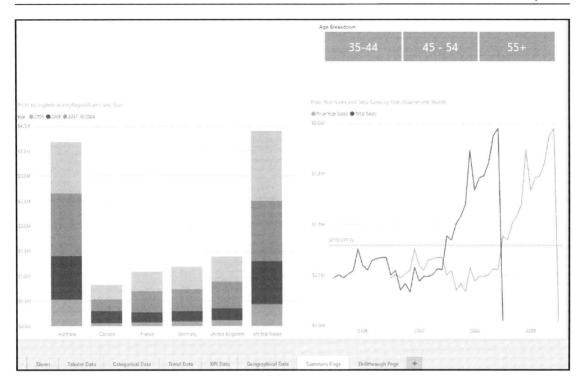

Figure 6.3-Visual representation at the Summary Page

With the visuals that we have put in place, we can start to create bookmarks. There are a couple of different approaches that can be adopted. The first option we will look at is simply filtering the data to a specific state and then selecting the **Add** option inside of the **Bookmarks** pane. Let's go ahead and select the option of **35–44** from the slicer to filter the page. Creating a bookmark for this really isn't impactful because this is something that users can do by themselves with a visual slicer, but we can use some of the other features in combination with this to create a specialized view of the data—for instance, the **Spotlight** option. Select the ellipsis in the upper right-hand corner of the **Stacked Column Chart** visual and choose the **Spotlight** option, which will fade all other visuals on the page. Now we can go ahead and select the **Add** option inside of the **Bookmarks** pane and rename the bookmark as **Spotlight Column 35–44**.

In order to rename the bookmark, you just need to select the ellipsis to the right of the newly created item. You will see the **Rename** option, along with many others, as shown in *Figure 6.4*:

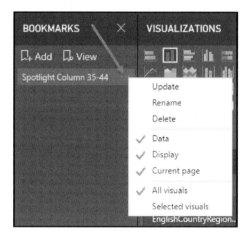

Figure 6.4

Let's take a moment to talk about what these options mean and how they will affect the bookmark:

- **Update:** With the bookmark selected, if any changes are made to the visuals, you can simply choose this option and the current state of the page will be saved for the selected bookmark.
- **Rename:** This option allows you to rename the selected bookmark.
- **Delete:** This option removes the currently selected bookmark.
- **Data:** If this option is checked, it will retain all the data properties from when this bookmark was created, such as the slicers or filters. Effectively, the visual will always reset the data to the state of when the bookmark was captured whenever it is selected. By deselecting this option, there will be no resetting of the filters when this bookmark is selected.
- **Display:** This option will retain visual properties, such as the **Spotlight** feature and the visibility.
- **Current page:** When this option is turned off, the bookmark page is effectively disabled, unless you are on the same page that the bookmark is referencing.
- **All visuals:** If this option is selected, then all visuals on the page, both visible and hidden, are part of the bookmark.
- **Selected visuals:** If this option is selected, then only the visuals that are selected when the bookmark is created will be stored.

As you can see from these many options, there are many different behaviors that we can choose to use with bookmarks. Now let's look at how bookmarks are best displayed. Go ahead select any area in the report page where there are no visuals. This will deselect the bookmark. Switch the slicer filter to **45–54** and once again use the **Spotlight** feature on the **Stacked Column Chart** and create another bookmark called **Spotlight Column 45–54**. Let's go ahead and add a third bookmark following the same steps, but pointing to the **55+** option within the slicer. This one should be called **Spotlight Column 55+**. Users can now open the **Bookmark** pane and choose to view whichever option they would like very easily, but we can also set this to a view mode that works well for presentations. Just next to the **Add** button, you will see an option called **View**, which will bring up some new icons at the bottom of the report page. As seen in *Figure 6.5*, we can now have a forward and back arrow, which allows us to move through all the available bookmarks and really tell a tailored story of the data. Also, while in this mode, all of the visuals are still completely available to be interacted with. To exit simply choose the **X** icon next to the arrows at the bottom or the **Exit** option within the **Bookmarks** pane, as shown in the following screenshot:

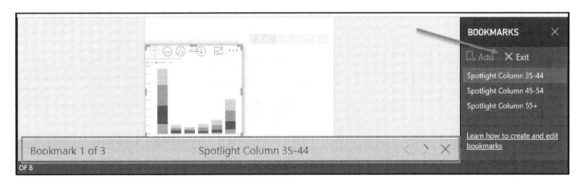

Figure 6.5

Even though we have already seen many different ways to use bookmarks, there are still more. Another fantastic way to guide report consumers to these tailored views of the data is by using images to link to these bookmarks. To get a better understanding of how to accomplish this, we must look at the **Selection** pane.

Selection pane

Also located under the **View** ribbon, we will find the **Selection** pane directly underneath the **Bookmarks** pane, and all we need to do is place a check mark inside the box. Immediately, you will see that another window will appear directly next to the **Bookmarks** pane. This pane provides a list of all the objects on the current page, and allows the user to decided whether a specific visual will be visible or not. This will allow us to efficiently use the space given to us within the report page. To demonstrate this, go ahead and make a duplicate of the **Stacked Column Chart** we currently have in the **Summary Page**. With this duplicate visual selected, let's change it to a **Table** visual and move it so that it lies directly on top of the column chart. Initially, it will look a little chaotic. You will see that this new visual is showing up in the **Selection** pane at the very bottom. In my example, it is called **Table**. Just to the right of this object, inside of the **Selection** pane, you will see an eye icon. By selecting this icon, you will see that the table visual disappears—it is still part of the report page, but has been hidden. Let's add a new bookmark and call it **Column View**. Also, for this new **Column View** bookmark, let's ensure that the **Data** option is not selected, as shown in *Figure 6.6*:

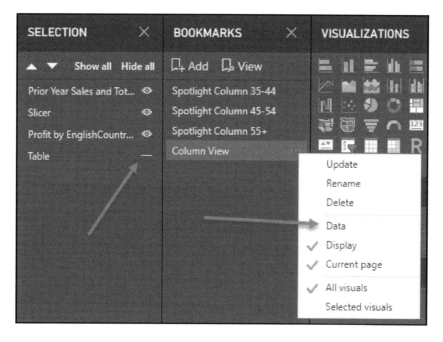

Figure 6.6

Let's create just one more bookmark, where we show the **Table** visual and instead hide the **Stacked Column Chart** visual. We will call this bookmark **Table View**, and it should also have the **Data** option deselected. We can now see that we have two different ways of displaying the same data within the same report page, really making the most of the space we have available. Also, there is another method that we can use to provide our users the ability to select between these two bookmarks using images, which is very exciting! Under the **Home** ribbon, you will find an option that says **Image**. This will launch a file browser to select an image file. For our example, navigate to `C:\Packt\Misc` and you will see two images: one that shows **Column** highlighted and the other showing **Table**. Bring both of these visuals into the **Summary Page** and, to the best of your ability, stack them on top of each other. To more easily distinguish the two images within the **Selection** pane, choose the image that has **Table** highlighted and turn on the **Title** option from the **Format Image** area, as shown in *Figure 6.7*. You will see in *Figure 6.7* that, after naming the object **Table Image**, the **Title** option was turned off, but now we can easily distinguish between the two images:

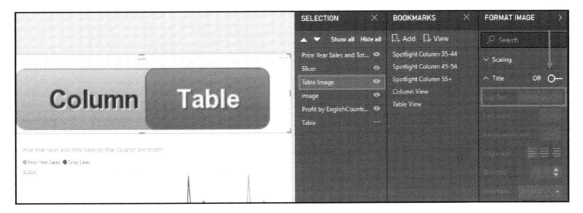

Figure 6.7-Table View bookmark

Now we can make it so that when our users click on this image, it will take us to the designated bookmark. So, for our example, we need to make a couple of quick updates to the **Column View** and **Table View** bookmarks. Let's begin by selecting the **Column View** bookmark and then hiding the object from the **Selection** pane labeled **Table Image**. Once this has been done, you can select the ellipsis for the **Column View** bookmark and choose the **Update** option. We now need to make the same change for the **Table View** bookmark by hiding the **Stacked Column Chart** visual and the **Image** object while making the **Table** and the **Table Image** object visible. Don't forget to choose the **Update** option once you have made the listed changes. The last piece that will tie all of this together is to assign an **Action** to the appropriate image within our bookmarks. While we still have the **Table View** bookmark selected, highlight the **Table Image** object and you will see an option within the **Format Image** area called **Action**. By expanding this **Action** area, you will see that we can change the **Type** selection, choose the **Bookmark** option, and then specify which bookmark the image will point to. The correct option in this situation would be choosing the **Column View** bookmark, as shown in *Figure 6.8*:

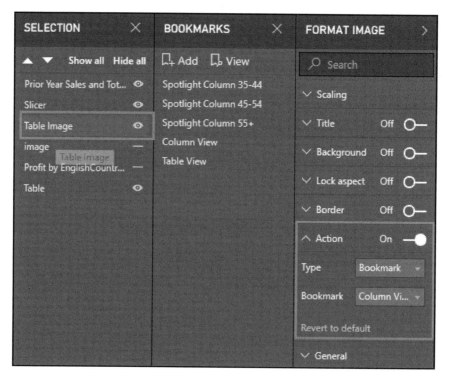

Figure 6.8

We have now made it so that when a user clicks on the **Table Image** object, we will be taken to the **Column View** bookmark. This makes our static image feel like an interactive button. In order to experience this behavior while developing the report, just hold the *Ctrl* key on the keyboard and left-click the image, and you will be taken to the **Column View** bookmark. To finish off this example, let's make the same changes to the **Column View** bookmark and set the **Image** object to have an **Action** that will point back to the **Table View** bookmark. Now we have set the behavior so that our users can freely choose how they will look at the data while making the most of the space within the report page. Hopefully, with these examples you can start to see the depth of what can be achieved by using the **Selection** pane and **Bookmarks** pane features for your digital storytelling.

Summary

We have taken a thorough journey through the various visuals that are at our disposal, and we have looked at the many features that allow us to tell exciting stories about our data. In the next chapter, we will discuss how we can take this completed Power BI report and deploy it so that we can share our hard work with others.

7
Using a Cloud Deployment with the Power BI Service

You've spent the course of this book creating amazing reports using the Power BI Desktop client. Now, it's time to share those reports with your team, company, or customers. In this chapter, you're going to learn about the Power BI service and how to use it to do the following:

- Deploy reports to the Power BI service
- Create and interact with dashboards
- Share dashboards
- Secure your reports with row-level security
- Schedule refreshes of your data

The Power BI service operates a freemium model. You can get most of the features in the free model, but when you want to share data with others and use team development, it will need to be upgraded to the pro edition. Other features requiring the pro edition are the ability to store larger datasets and more frequently refresh, to name a few.

 Before you begin this chapter, make sure you sign up for a free account at PowerBI (https://powerbi.microsoft.com/). Some sections of this book will require a pro license, such as the section dealing with workspaces.

Deploying to the Power BI service

There are numerous ways to publish a report to the `PowerBI.com` service, but the easiest way is by using the Power BI desktop. To do this, you'll need to simply click the **Publish** button in the desktop application, as shown in the following screenshot. If you have not previously signed in with your free PowerBI.com account, you will be prompted to create one or sign in with an existing account:

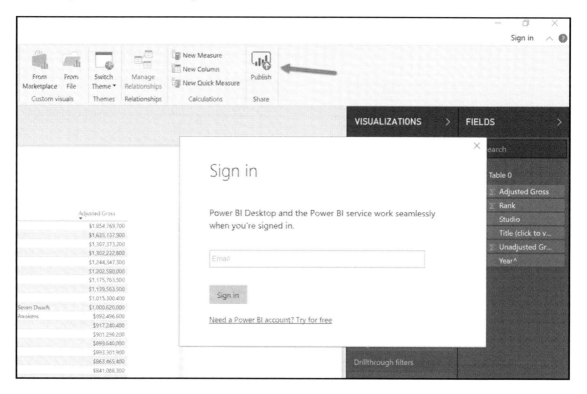

You'll then be asked which workspace you want to deploy to. A *workspace* is an area in the Power BI service that is much like a folder, where you can bundle your reports, datasets, and dashboards. You can also assign security to the workspace and not have to worry about securing each item. Most importantly, it allows for team development of a Power BI solution, where you can have multiple authors on a solution. We'll cover much more about workspaces in the *Sharing Your Dashboards* section of this chapter.

At this point, select the **My Workspace** item, which will send the report and its data to your personal workspace. The report will then deploy to the Power BI service. The amount of time this takes will depend on how large your dataset is. You'll then be presented with two options: **Open the Report** or **Get Quick Insights**.

Quick Insights is an amazing feature in Power BI that will try to find additional interesting insights about your data that you may not have known you had. For example, in the following screenshot of the sample report, it found that Disney dominated all other film studios in 2016. You'll notice that it not only provides a graphic of the anomaly in your data, but also a narrative to the right of the graphic. If you find any of the insights especially interesting, you can click the push pin on the top right of the graphic to save it into a dashboard. We'll cover dashboards in the next section of this chapter:

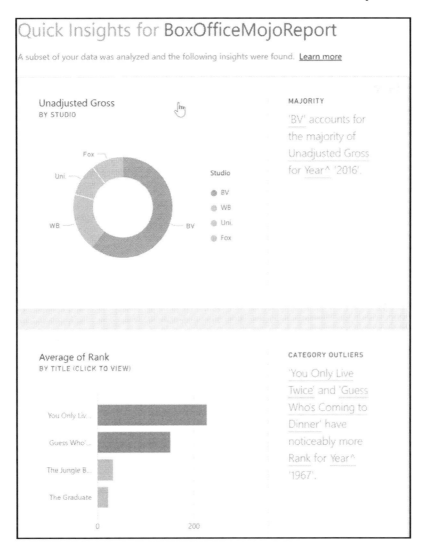

If you open the report, `PowerBI.com` will launch and show you the same report that you were viewing in the desktop in a web browser. You'll also be able to immediately see the report in the Power BI mobile app from your Android or iPhone. `PowerBI.com` has four key areas that you can interact with:

- **DATASETS**: This is the raw data that you have built in the Power BI desktop. You can also build a new dataset by clicking **Get Data** in the bottom-left corner of your browser. When you click the datasets, you can also build new reports from those dataset.
- **WORKBOOKS**: You can upload Excel workbooks into this area. These Excel workbooks can be used as a dataset or can form pieces of the workbook that can be pinned to a dashboard.
- **REPORTS**: This refers to what you have built in the Power BI desktop. These reports can be explored, modified, or downloaded in this section.
- **DASHBOARDS**: You can pin the best elements from multiple reports into a unified set of dashboards. These dashboards are the first thing most of your casual users will interact with:

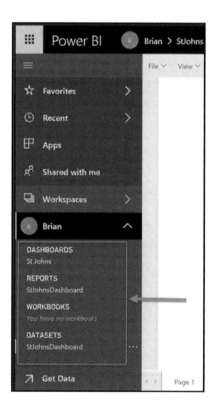

DATASETS

The **DATASETS** area of Power BI holds the raw data that makes up your reports. When you left-click on one of your datasets, the designer opens to build reports from the dataset. The designer can be used to do the following things:

- Create more Quick Insights
- Create new reports
- Refresh or schedule refreshes
- Manage permissions
- Download the Power BI Desktop file (.pbix)

When you start with a dataset, users can create new reports from your data, even when accessing it through the web. The entire user interface will feel nearly identical to Power BI Desktop, but you will be lacking the ability to modify the model, query, and relationships. The best part of building reports here is that you have a central dataset that IT can own, modify, and make human-readable so that the entire organization can build reports off of it.

WORKBOOKS

The **WORKBOOKS** section gives you the ability to upload Excel workbooks, which can be used as datasets for a report or to pin selected parts of that workbook to a dashboard. Workbooks can be updated by either reuploading the workbook, using the database management gateway, or using OneDrive. OneDrive is Microsoft's cloud-hosted hard drive system. With OneDrive, you can simply share or save your Excel workbooks, and if you're using the workbook in a Power BI report, it can also refresh.

Creating and interacting with dashboards

Once you have deployed your datasets and are using them in reports, you're ready to bring together the many report elements into a single dashboard. Often, your management team is going to want to have a unified executive dashboard that combines elements such as your sales numbers, bank balances, customer satisfaction scores, and more into a single dashboard. The amazing thing about dashboards in Power BI is that data can be actionable and reacted to quickly. You can click on any dashboard element and be immediately taken to the report that makes up that number. You can also subscribe to the dashboard and create mobile alerts when certain numbers on the dashboard reach a milestone.

Creating your first dashboard

To create your first dashboard, start by opening a report that has some interesting data. On each of the charts, tiles, and other elements, you'll see a pin icon in the top right of that object. After you click on the pin, it will ask you what dashboard you wish to pin that report element to. You can, at that point, select a new dashboard to create or choose an existing dashboard to add the element to, as shown in the following screenshot. This is what makes Power BI so magical—you're able to append data from your accounting department next to data from your sales and customer service teams, giving your executives one place to look:

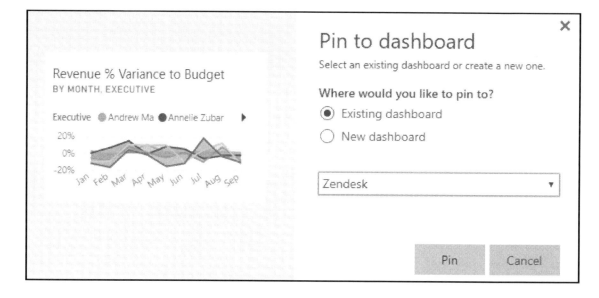

Once you pin the first item to the dashboard, you'll be prompted with a link to the dashboard. The newly created dashboard will allow you to resize elements and add additional tiles of information. You can click **Add Tile** in the upper-right corner to add additional interesting data, such as web content, images—such as logos—text data, and videos to the dashboard. Most people use this in the line-manager dashboard to insert a company logo and a small video talking about the initiative of the quarter that relates to the dashboard from the executive team.

You can also pin real-time data as a tile, as well use custom streaming data. Once you click **Custom Streaming Dataset**, you have the option to add a new dataset from Azure Stream Analytics or PubNub, or a developer can use the API to push data directly in via the API. Azure Stream Analytics is the most common of these live data streams. In this mechanism, devices could stream data through Azure Event Hub, for example, and then get aggregated with Azure Stream Analytics. Imagine a smart power grid sending thousands of records a second to the cloud, and then Azure Stream Analytics aggregating this to a single record every five seconds, the status shown by a moving needle in a gauge or line graph in Power BI.

One of the key ways to view Power BI is from a phone either in web view or in the native Power BI client, which is downloadable from the App Store for Android or iPhone. There are going to be some dashboard elements that you'll want to exclude from a phone device because the surface area is too small. By the very nature of the device, most people sign into Power BI on their phone to get a quick look at the numbers. For those consumers, you can create a specialized phone view of the dashboard.

Simply click on the **Web View** drop-down box in the top right and select **Phone View**. The default phone view will contain every element from the web view. To remove items, hover over each report element and click the push pin to move it to the **Unpinned Tiles** section, as shown in the following screenshot. Once you're done, you can click the phone icon (or **Phone View** name, based on your resolution) and flip it back to the **Web View** again:

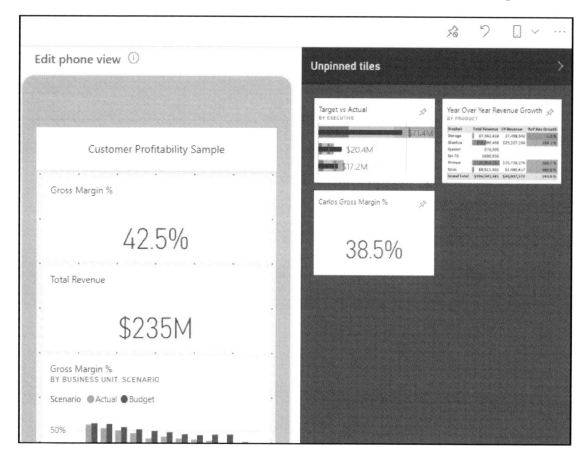

Asking your dashboard a question

Once the dashboard is complete, you're able to ask questions of your data. Right above the dashboards' data, you'll see the area where you can **Ask a question about your data**. For example, you can ask the question "Show me the total stores by state", and Power BI will typically produce a geography answer from that question. If you'd prefer to see your answer as a bar chart instead of a map, you can explicitly ask for it as a graph element—for example, "Show me the total stores by state in a bar chart".

If you like the answer that comes back, you can click **Pin Visual** in the top-right corner to pin the report item to a dashboard. You can also expand the **Filters** and **Visualizations** on the right to be very precise with your report item. For example, you may only want to see stores with sales above a certain level. While Power BI is great at answering questions with filters, it sometimes needs fine tuning. If you're curious as to where Power BI pulled this data from, below your newly created report, you'll see the source of the data from which the report was derived.

A great way to encourage your users to utilize this feature is to seed Power BI with some sample questions. To do this, select the settings gear box on the upper-right corner of your screen. Once there, click the dataset that you wish to create sample questions for in the **Datasets** tab, as shown in the following screenshot. Expand the **Featured Q&A Questions** section, click **Add a Question,** and add several questions that might interest your user:

Creating featured questions will help your users to start to use the vocabulary of the report. For example, your sales team may be used to calling someone a "client", but your marketing team uses the term "customer". Featured questions will encourage all users to refer to customers as clients. If you want to have your cake and eat it too, you can create synonyms inside the Power BI desktop. You can do this in the modeling tab when looking at your relationships. You can also create more advanced linguistic models in the Power BI desktop by importing linguistic models. This can help with questions that you think users might ask, such as "Who is my best customer in New York?" or "Show me the worst employees by office." The linguistic model would translate what "best" and "worst" means to the company.

One of the amazing features you can do inside of Power BI is to ask questions through Cortana, Windows's voice-operated assistant. With Cortana integration enabled in the **Settings** tab, your users will be able to ask questions in Windows without logging into Power BI, and can get quick answers right from the **Start** menu. To do this, the user must have their company account (typically Office 365) associated with Windows by going to **Settings** | **Account** in Windows. You must also connect Office 365 to Cortana as a connected service.

Subscribing to reports and dashboards

To discourage users from printing reports and dashboards, you can have them subscribe to the reports and dashboards instead. This will email the report or dashboard when the data changes on the report, typically daily or weekly. Select **Subscribe** in the upper-right corner of the browser. Power BI will read the account you're signed in with and subscribe you using that email address. When subscribing to reports, you must select the report page that you wish to be emailed to you. With dashboards, the entire dashboard will be emailed.

You can also set up alerts from your mobile device to alert you when a critical number changes on a report. While looking at a dashboard, you can click the alert icon (it looks like a bell) to create an alert. This will monitor the data on the report, and upon that number hitting a certain threshold, it will send you a phone alert and, optionally, an additional email. Alerts are great mechanisms to let you know if a given critical number, such as a profit margin, has fallen.

Subscriptions and alerts can be managed in the Power BI settings area under the **Alerts** and **Subscriptions** tabs. You can turn off alerts and subscriptions here, as well as edit the subscriptions. By default, the frequency of subscriptions will be whenever the data is updated, but this happens typically no more than once per day (although this can be altered).

Sharing your dashboards

Sharing in Power BI is quite simple, but you'll want to consider what your goal is first. If your goal is simply to share a view-only version of a report or dashboard that users could engage with, the basic sharing mechanism can do that. If your goal is instead to allow users to also edit the report, you will want to use workspaces. Lastly, if you want to logically package reports and dashboards together, and have the ability to have fine-control over which reports can be seen by default, consider using Power BI apps.

The easiest way to share a dashboard or report is to simply click **Share** in the upper-right corner of any report or dashboard. Simply type the email address of the user that you want to share with and what type of access you want to give them. While you can't allow them to edit the report or dashboard, they will be able to view and reshare the report themselves. At any time, you can also see what assets are shared with you by clicking **Shared with Me** from the left menu. Then, you will see a list of users that have shared items with you. You can click on this list to filter the report lists that are shared with you.

Workspaces

Workspaces are areas where groups of users can collaborate with datasets, reports, and dashboards. You can create a workspace if you have a pro license of the Power BI service. This is the main way that your BI developers will be able to codevelop the same sets of data and reports. Typically, you'll create a workspace for each department in your company for the teams to store their items and data.

To create one, simply expand the **Workspaces** section in the left navigation menu and click **Create App Workspace**. Name the workspace that you wish to create and define whether members can edit the content or just view the content, as shown in the following screenshot. You can also define whether users will be able to see the content of what's inside the workspace without being a member. This doesn't mean they'll be able to see the reports, but they will be able to see the metadata. If you're running the Power BI premium edition, you can also assign the dedicated capacity to a given workspace.

This is handy for those executive reports that must always return their visuals in a few seconds:

 At any time, you can change the permissions or add users by editing the workspace if you have permission to do so. To do this, select the ellipsis button next to the workspace name and click **Edit Workspace**.

Setting up row-level security

In most organizations, security is not just a report-level decision. Organizations want more granular decisions, such as whether a sales executive can only see his or her own data. Another example is the ability for a teacher to see his or her own students, but the school's principal can see all the teachers at their school and the school board members can see all of the data. This level of granularity is quite possible in Power BI, but will require some thought ahead of time on how to lay the data out.

To show an example of this, we'll need to go back to the Power BI Desktop and open Chapter 5 - Visualizing Data Completed.pbix from a previous chapter's example; this file can be downloaded from this book's web page at http://packtpub.com. The goal of this example is to ensure that United States sales managers can only see US sales, and likewise for Australian sales managers. We'll only use two countries in our example, but the same example can apply to the entire world, and can be expanded to be made more dynamic.

To create this type of automated filter based on your user's credentials, you'll need to use DAX language snippets. Open the Power BI Desktop and click **Manage Roles** from the **Modeling** ribbon in the report. Then, click **Create** to make a new role called **US**. Then, select **Sales Territory** as your table to filter on and click **Add Filter | [Sales Territory Country]**, as shown in the following screenshot. This will create a stub of code in the **Table Filter DAX Expression** box that shows **[Sales Territory Country] = Value**. Simply replace **Value** with **United States**, and your first role is created. Do the same for Australia to complete the example:

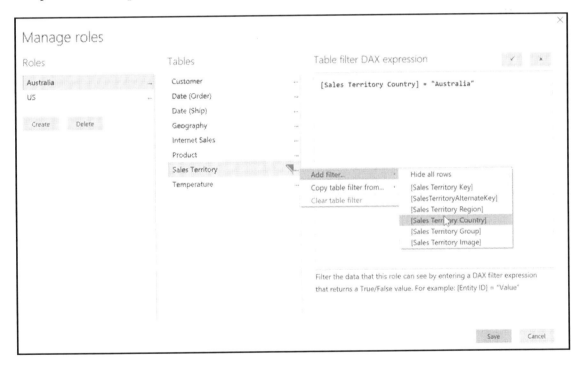

Now that we've created the two rules, let's test them out. The Power BI desktop will not automatically filter the data for you, since you have access to the underlying data anyway, but it can be used to test it. Click **View as Role** from the **Modeling** tab and select the role you wish to test. You'll notice after you click on Australia, for example, that every report element on each report page filters at that point to only show Australian data. Power BI Desktop also warns you that you're filtering the data, and that you can click **Stop Viewing** to stop viewing as the role. Once you're ready to see what you've done on the Power BI service, publish to your Power BI account and open the report there.

Navigate to the dataset matching your report and select **Security**. You can then select each role and type the email address of each member of that role. Click **Add** and then **Save** to start using the role, as shown in the following screenshot. You can also add groups (such as your Australian Employee group) to this role if you have one created already in Office 365's directory. After clicking **Save**, members of that role will only see their own data in dashboards, reports, and any new reports that they build from the dataset:

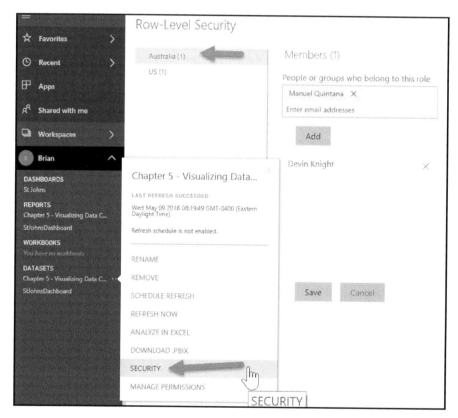

If your user has edit rights to the workspace or dataset, then these roles will not work since they already have the ability to see the underlying data. However, roles do work if the user is connecting to Power BI Desktop to see the data through Excel. Make sure the members of the workspace only have **View** rights selected if this feature is important to you. Additionally, when row-level security is turned on, Q&A will no longer work as of the publication of this book.

Scheduling data refreshes

Once you have a report that everyone depends on, you're not going to want to refresh it manually each day. The Power BI service has the ability to refresh your datasets up to every half an hour for the Power BI pro edition when you're not doing real-time analysis. If all of your data lives in the cloud, refreshing is very simple. However, if you have some data or files on premise, you must install the on-premises gateway.

Don't forget that if you want to see data in real time, you have the option to perform a direct query, where clicks run queries against your source system. Doing this will slow your reports down by large factors. You can also do real-time analysis of your data by using Azure services, such as Stream Analytics, where elements in your dashboards refresh every second.

The on-premises gateways can be used across multiple cloud services, such as Power BI, PowerApps, Logic Apps, and Microsoft Flow. You can download the free gateway from the top-right download icon on PowerBI.com once you're signed in. The first question that will be asked during the installation is whether you want to install the data gateway in personal mode or on-premises gateway mode.

The largest difference between the on-premises data gateway and the on-premises data gateway in personal mode is that personal mode runs as an application versus a Windows service. By installing in personal mode, you risk your data becoming stale if the application is not open when your PC starts. It is handy for those users who may not have admin access to their machine, or users who want easier data refreshes. It is recommended for ease of management and reliability that most users install the on-premises data gateway.

After installation, you'll need to provide your Power BI login credentials. Next, you'll need to name your gateway and provide a recovery key, as shown in the following screenshot. The recovery key is used to encrypt your connection strings and your configuration. Make sure that this key is kept in a safe place and is backed up. If you wish to make this gateway highly available, you can add the gateway into a cluster, allowing multiple machines to act as a single gateway to Power BI:

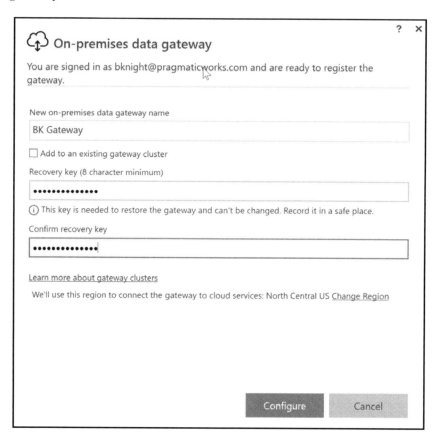

With the on-premises work now complete, you will need to complete the configuration on PowerBI.com. Click the settings gear box from the top-right corner and select **Manage Gateways**. At that point, you should see the gateways on the left. You can add more administrators (who have permission to configure data sources that can use this connection) in the **Administrators** tab.

Most importantly, you will want to test the gateway before proceeding.

Now, we need to create a connection to each of your files or databases that are used in your report that are on-premises. Click the **Add Data Source** button from the top-left corner. Give the data source a name that can enable you to easily identify it later. Typically, that name should match the filename or database name to help with debugging later. For Excel files or any other type of files used in your report, select **File** from the **Data Source Type** drop-down box. Then, type the full path for the filename or a network path (UNC path). Lastly, give the Windows credentials that are needed to access the file on the share or folder. Once you're finalized, click **Test all Connections** again to ensure you have a proper connection, as shown in the following screenshot:

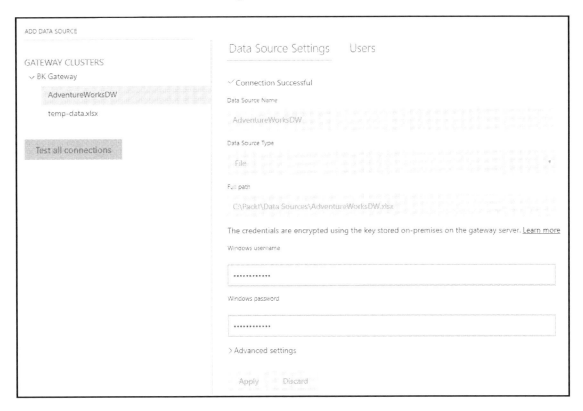

The **Users** tab also allows you to have more refined control of who can access this data source. Once you've saved those settings, you're ready to schedule the refresh. If you wish to just refresh the data immediately, select the ellipsis button next to the dataset and select **Refresh Now**. To schedule a refresh, click **Schedule Refresh**. This will take you to the dataset configuration screen. Expand the **Gateway Connection** section, select **Use an On-Prem Data Gateway**, and click **Apply**. You should see your gateway name in this section, with a status reading **Online**. If you don't see **Online**, check whether there are any proxy settings or firewall issues preventing Power BI from seeing your machine.

Next, expand the **Scheduled Refresh** section in this **Datasets** tab and switch the setting **Keep Your Data Up to Date** to **On**. You can then schedule the refresh to occur as often as every half an hour. Once you test the refresh, you can see the **Refresh History** in this same tab to see whether the data was successfully refreshed. You can also get email notifications of when refreshing fails.

If your data is already in Azure or OneDrive, then the on-premises gateway is not required. You just need to make sure the firewall will allow you to communicate with the Power BI service.

Summary

The Power BI service allows your users to see the same reports on a web or mobile platform with the same type of interactivity as they experience in Power BI Desktop. It also allows users to build reports quickly, straight from a web platform. Once your reports are deployed to the service, you can use row-level security to see data at a granular level, allowing a sales manager to only see their own territory. The data can also be refreshed every 30 minutes. If you're using on-premises data sources, then you can use the on-premises gateway to bring data from on premise to the cloud.

8

On-Premises Solutions with Power BI Report Server

Throughout this book, we've focused on building reports that would ultimately be deployed to the web through the Power BI service or shown in the mobile application. In this chapter, we'll show you how to deploy reports to Power BI Report Server, which is likely being hosted on premises at your company. For many companies, this is a must-have, since cloud deployments are often not allowed with their type of data or industry.

Power BI Report Server is an on-premises version of the Power BI service that gives you a subset of the features of the full service. Just like the service, which is sometimes daily updated with new features, the Power BI Service is updated every few months. There is also an additional Power BI desktop specially made for the server.

 Make sure you fully explore the features of the server to ensure it has the critical features that you love. For example, you might find that a connector you can use in the Power BI service is not available in the server. The biggest notable missing feature is the lack of dashboards.

Deploying to Power BI Report Server

If you're a traditional BI developer who has built Reporting Services reports, you might feel right at home with Power BI Report Server, as the configuration and portals were largely borrowed from Reporting Services. The main difference is that you will not use Visual Studio to build reports. You're going to use a special Power BI desktop that is optimized for the server. The main reason for the separate desktop is to ensure that the desktop doesn't promote a feature that the server does not support. One key advantage to using this approach is that Report Server can also host your traditional Reporting Services reports, KPIs, and mobile reports.

Before deploying your report, you may want to create some folders to simplify finding your reports later. For example, creating a folder for finance, HR, inventory, IT, operations, and sales is a common starting point. Don't worry: you can always move the reports later if you've already deployed them. Once you've created a folder, if you feel it's needed, you can deploy your Power BI reports in one of two ways: from the Power BI desktop or by uploading.

Make sure you have an Power BI desktop installed that supports Power BI Server and open the report that you wish to deploy. This flavor of Power BI Desktop also supports deploying to the cloud if you need a single experience, but note that you will be at least 3–4 months behind the main Power BI application. Next, click **File** | **Save As** | **Power BI Server**. If this is your first time deploying your report to the server, everything will be blank. Simply type the Report Server HTTP address in the box to connect to the Power BI Server. It should look something like `http://servername/reports`. If you have a port number, you'll need to use something like `http://servername:portnumber/reports`. You can find the exact location to enter by going to your Report Server Configuration Manager tool from the server and copying the URL from the **Web Portal URL** section. The port in this screenshot is port 80, which you don't have to enter as it is the default port:

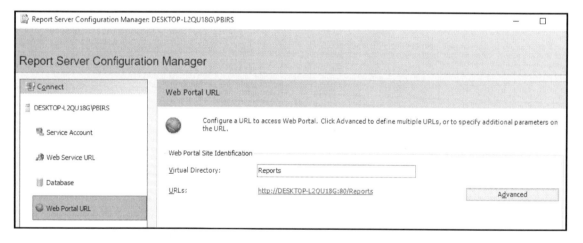

If the desktop can successfully connect to the server, you will be prompted for the folder name that you want to deploy to and the name of the report you want to use. Typically, you don't want to use this opportunity to change the name of the report since it will become difficult to find your source report later. After clicking **OK**, the report will deploy and provide you a link that will take you directly to the report that now resides on your server. From this point forward, you can click **Save** without going through this process and it will save directly to the server.

You can also upload the report directly in the browser. To do this, simply go to the folder you wish to upload the report to and click **Upload** in the top-right corner. You will then be prompted for the location of the folder, and then you're done. Power BI Server will scan to make sure that the report is compatible. For example, if you built the report on a very new version of Power BI Desktop that is using features that aren't supported in Power BI Server yet, then you will receive an error before the upload occurs. Once the report is deployed, any user with the appropriate access can also click the **Edit** button in Power BI Desktop to open the report up in the desktop so that they can make changes.

If you wish to move the report to a new folder, you can go to the report listing and click **Move** under the ellipsis button. You will be prompted for the folder you wish to move the report to, and then you're done. You can also do this under **Manage** in the same ellipsis.

In the **Manage** area of a report, you can also hide the report by clicking **Hide this Object**. This can be used to hide reports that are built on other reports, for example. It's important to note, though, that this is not a security mechanism. There's nothing to stop a user from seeing the report if they unhide the object.

Securing reports

You can secure a report in the **Manage** screen of a report or folder. To access this area, select a report folder or report, select the ellipsis button, and click **Manage**. Then, go to the **Security** tab. By default, reports and folders inherit security from their parent folder, but this can be undone quickly by clicking **Customize Security**.

Keep in mind that there's quite a bit of overlap in the roles that can be assigned, mainly due to the context of what you're securing (**My Reports** or the public folder or reports). The security roles that you can select are listed as follows:

- **Browser**: Can view the reports and folders, and subscribe to the reports
- **Content Manager**: Can manage folders, reports, and resources
- **My Reports**: Can publish reports and manage folders, reports, and resources in a user's `My Reports` folder
- **Publisher**: Can publish reports on your Power BI Report Server
- **Report Builder**: Can review any definitions or metadata about the report

You can also select the gear box in the top-right corner of the screen and select **Site Settings** to secure the entire server. Even if you have rights to the folder or report, you may not have rights to the server, which creates a lot of confusion with system administrators and users trying to view their data. When you go to **Site Settings**, you can add a user to one of two roles: **System Administrator** or **System User**. The system administrator can manage the security on the server and the schedules, to name just a few options. The system user grants the user rights to log in to the server, and then requires security to view the folders and reports, as shown earlier in this section.

Scheduling data refreshes

Refreshing data in Power BI Report Server comes with a lot more caveats than using the Power BI cloud service. For example, refreshing is contingent on the data source that the report is using. Since you've installed this server inside your firewall, there's no need for a data management gateway to refresh the data either. As you create refreshing schedules, the server will simply create SQL Server Agent jobs to control the refreshes, such as Reporting Services. Because of this, SQL Agent must be started in order to create scheduled refreshes.

If you plan on refreshing data sources that are derived from files, make sure you use a network path for that file (\\computername\sharename\file.csv), not a local path (such as C:\Downloads\File.csv). You can do this in Power BI Desktop by going to the **Home** ribbon and selecting **Edit Queries** | **Data Source Settings**. Click **Change Source** and change any file references to a network path, such as \\MyComputer\c$\Downloads\File.csv.

Once you do that, publish the report to the server again. Then, select the report and select **Manage**. For most data sources, you will need to confirm the **Data Sources** tab. For flat files, confirm that you see the network path and type in the credentials for the machine that's holding those files. This will need to be a Windows Authentication username and password. Click **Test Connection** to confirm that a connection can be successfully achieved. If it tests successfully, click **Save**.

> If you find that there are popular times at which people want to refresh data, you can create shared schedules. Shared schedules can be found in the **Site Settings** administration panel (under the gear box in the top-right corner) of the portal. By creating these, you will simplify the scheduling of future jobs for popular schedule times.

To schedule the refresh, click **Scheduled Refresh** in the report management area. Then, click **New Scheduled Refresh Plan** to create a new schedule. You can also use a shared schedule resource or a one-off schedule. Simply type the time you wish the refresh to occur and the refresh interval. While there are workarounds, the lowest grain of a scheduled refresh is typically hourly.

Test the job by selecting the job and clicking **Refresh Now**. If any errors occur, you will see the error inline in the **Status** column. For example, the following error would show as a `Data source error: Login failed for data source 'Unknown'`. This is not nearly enough information to debug with, so click the information icon next to the error to see a more actionable error, such as the following:

```
[0] -1055784932: Could not find file '\\desktop-
12qu18g\c$\OneDrive\Documents\CountyClerksFL.csv'.. The exception was
raised by the IDbCommand interface.
```

Summary

In this short chapter, you learned how to take the Power BI Service practices on site with the Power BI Server. This server has many restrictions on what's available, so be careful that you have the right version of the desktop so that it matches your version of the server. As you've learned, the server resembles the Reporting Services server and uses SQL Server Agent to handle data refreshes.

Other Books You May Enjoy

If you enjoyed this book, you may be interested in these other books by Packt:

Microsoft Power BI Cookbook
Brett Powell

ISBN: 978-1-78829-014-2

- Cleanse, stage, and integrate your data sources with Power BI
- Abstract data complexities and provide users with intuitive, self-service BI capabilities
- Build business logic and analysis into your solutions via the DAX programming language and dynamic, dashboard-ready calculations
- Take advantage of the analytics and predictive capabilities of Power BI
- Make your solutions more dynamic and user specific and/or defined including use cases of parameters, functions, and row level security
- Understand the differences and implications of DirectQuery, Live Connections, and Import-Mode Power BI datasets and how to deploy content to the Power BI Service and schedule refreshes
- Integrate other Microsoft data tools such as Excel and SQL Server Reporting Services into your Power BI solution

Mastering Microsoft Power BI
Brett Powell

ISBN: 978-1-78829-723-3

- Build efficient data retrieval and transformation processes with the Power Query M Language
- Design scalable, user-friendly DirectQuery and Import Data Models
- Develop visually rich, immersive, and interactive reports and dashboards
- Maintain version control and stage deployments across development, test, and production environments
- Manage and monitor the Power BI Service and the On-Premises Data Gateway
- Develop a fully On-Premise Solution with the Power BI Report Server
- Scale up a Power BI solution via Power BI Premium capacity and migration to Azure Analysis Services or SQL Server Analysis Services

Leave a review - let other readers know what you think

Please share your thoughts on this book with others by leaving a review on the site that you bought it from. If you purchased the book from Amazon, please leave us an honest review on this book's Amazon page. This is vital so that other potential readers can see and use your unbiased opinion to make purchasing decisions, we can understand what our customers think about our products, and our authors can see your feedback on the title that they have worked with Packt to create. It will only take a few minutes of your time, but is valuable to other potential customers, our authors, and Packt. Thank you!

Index